HART PICTURE ARCHIVES

Hart Publishing Company, Inc. • New York City

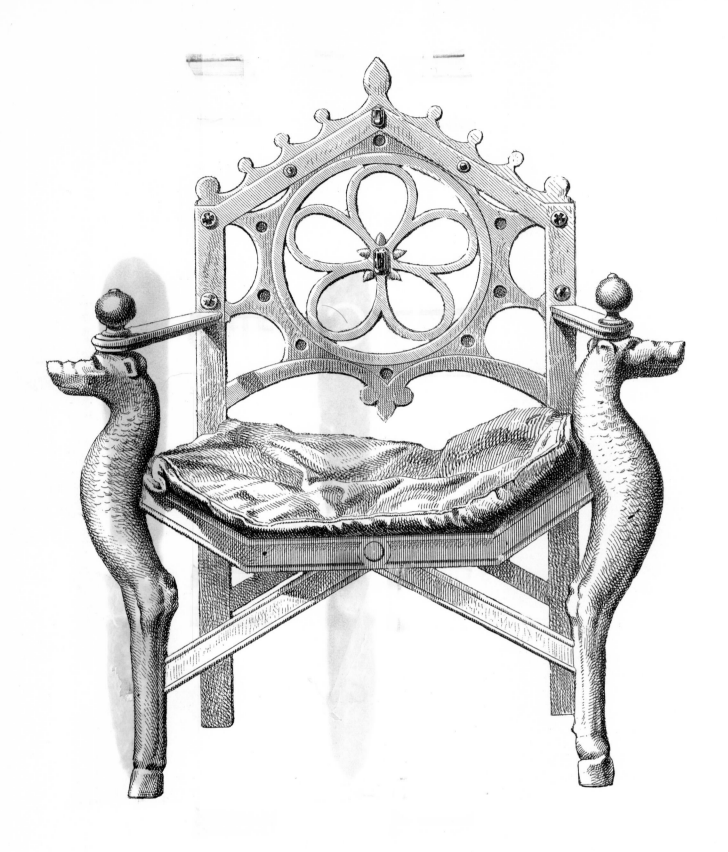

ISBN NO. 08055-1209-8 (Paperback 08055-0302-1)
LIBRARY OF CONGRESS CATALOG CARD NO. 76-54044

MANUFACTURED IN THE UNITED STATES OF AMERICA

CONTENTS

HOW TO USE THIS BOOK

CHAIRS is a collection of over 500 pictures of many periods, culled from 21 known sources. These pictures have been subdivided into 22 categories.

All these pictures are in the public domain. They derive from magazines, books, and pictures copyrighted by Hart Publishing Company, now released to the public for general use.

So as not to clutter a caption, the source of the picture is given an abbreviated designation. Full publication data may be found in the *Sources* section, in which all sources are listed in alphabetical order, with the full title of the book or magazine, the publisher, and the date of publication. The *Sources* section commences on page 142.

Captions appear only beneath those pictures which call for clear identification. For example, many pictures in the *Ancient* section are identified by their place of construction, as well as a description of the materials used.

One hundred twenty-two pictures are halftones, and are designated by a square symbol □ at the end of the caption. These pictures, too, are suitable for reproduction, but the user is alerted to rescreen such a picture or convert it into line. All other pictures can be reproduced directly in line.

The *Index* begins on page 143. All index entries set in full caps represent one of the 22 major groupings in this book.

Introduction

Simply defined, the chair is a seat designed to accommodate one person. But this bare definition cannot begin to explore the almost limitless variety of chairs. Of all pieces of furniture, the chair has been executed in the widest variety of forms, as the pictures in this book will confirm.

This volume contains 500 examples of designs representing the significant periods in the stylistic history of the chair. Included are the works of famous craftsmen—Hepplewhite, Sheraton, Chippendale, among others—as well as modern and unusual chairs.

It was not until the sixteenth century that the chair came into popular use. Previously, chairs were reserved for kings and ecclesiastical potentates, and thus were regarded as symbols of authority.

As an emblem of the state, the chair served a symbolic, as well as a utilitarian, purpose for thousands of years. This is manifest today in the manner in which we use the word *chair*. When the leader of an assembly announces "The chair recognizes _____," he is obviously not referring to a piece of furniture, but rather to the authority invested in him—symbolized by his chair.

Until the sixteenth century, common men sat on benches, stools, and chests. The bench was especially useful as it was easily constructed and could accommodate a large number of people. Crudely finished, benches were not upholstered or adorned in any way, and as they were usually backless, comfort was minimal. The stool, too, was simple to make, being fashioned from untrimmed forest timber. Stools had an advantage over benches in that they were portable. The chest served a variety of furnishing needs. Essentially a storage place for clothing and household objects, the chest was literally a box that could be sat upon.

The chair, on the other hand, was more elaborate and more comfortable than these crude seats; after all, it possessed a back and, sometimes, even arms and upholstery. But the earliest chairs were basically simple, especially when compared with the ever-more ornate specimens which developed.

Modern chair design has produced many new styles, however, not all have won public acceptance. Only within the past three decades has the ultra-modern chair become a standard furnishing item. The design of this contemporary chair dispenses with the conventional elements of decoration in favor of utter simplicity. Thus, ironically, the development of the chair has returned full cycle.

Ancient

Our knowledge of the chairs fashioned in remote antiquity is derived from monuments, sculpture, and paintings. Except for a few Egyptian chairs which are housed in museums in Cairo and the British Museum, few examples of ancient chairs exist.

The chairs of ancient Egypt appear to have been skillfully constructed and decorated with an unusual richness of material and design. They were fashioned of ebony and of ivory, often carved and gilded. Covered with costly fabrics, these chairs were supported by legs carved to resemble the hindquarters of beasts or the figures of captives.

From monuments excavated at Nineveh, it appears that chairs without backs were constructed and used in Assyria. These chairs were adorned with carved legs terminating in lions' claws or bulls' hooves. Other Assyrian chairs were supported by *caryatides* (representations of human figures) or the complete figures of animals.

The earliest Greek chairs for which we have evidence date back to the fifth or sixth century B.C.E. The back supports of these chairs are perpendicular to their seats. They do not curve to conform to the human spine, and no attempt has been made to provide comfort. Visitors to the Parthenon will find a representation of the Greek god Zeus on the frieze of that building. The deity occupies a square seat with thick-turned legs. This chair is ornamented with winged sphinxes and the feet of beasts. Despite the obvious attempt to seat Zeus on a throne befitting his eminence, no attempt has been made to provide for his comfort.

The *curule*, or folding chair, was a unique invention of ancient craftsmen. This chair, thought to have been originally placed in a magistrate's chariot, was often inlaid with ivory; it had curved legs and was usually backless. The name of this type of chair has been adopted into the English language and is used in the general sense of "an official." Though the design of the curule was generally simple, in the course of time it was ornamented and eventually relieved of its portable nature. Subsequently, Roman chairs were made of marble and adorned with sphinxes similar to the type appearing on their Greek counterparts. It is clear that chairs in ancient Rome were reserved for the nobility, and were fashioned for those who could afford extravagant materials and expensive artisans.

Perhaps the most famous chair still in existence is the chair of St. Peter housed in St. Peter's Cathedral in Rome. It is made of acacia wood but contains supportive restorations taken from an earlier chair made of oak. The wood is now severely damaged by decay. According to scholars, the chair was constructed during the sixth century in the Byzantine style. The labors of Hercules are represented in its ivory carvings. This precious chair, kept under triple lock, is exhibited only once every century.

Like Greece and Rome, Byzantium favored the curule as its most common form of seating. Lions' heads, figures of winged Victory, and dolphin-shaped arms were favored decorative devices. Often, the back of the chair was designed to resemble a lyre.

Repose of King Asshurbanipal. *History of Furniture*

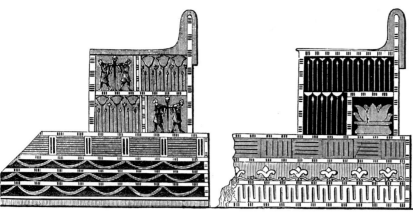

Egyptian thrones. *Zell's*

Roman judgment seat. *Harper's*

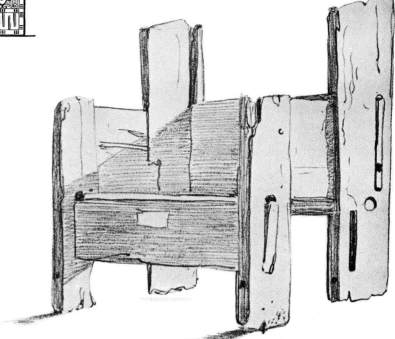

St. Augustine's chair, Canterbury. *Connoisseur, Vol. 38* □

Chair of Bishop Maximianus, Ravenna. *Litchfield*

Fresco representing a feast in ancient Egypt. *History of Furniture*

Ancient continued

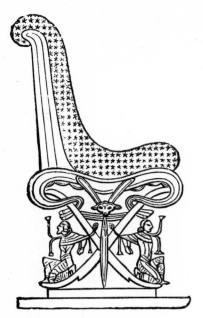

Egyptian chair. *Zell's*

Assyrian bronze throne and footstool, circa 888 B.C. *History of Furniture* □

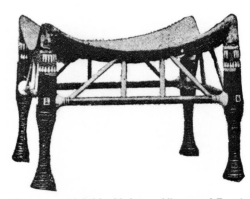

Ebony seat inlaid with ivory, *History of Furniture* □

Early folding stool. *Litchfield* □

A fragment of a wall painting depicting the seated figure
of a high-ranking Egyptian. *History of Furniture* □

White marble Etruscan seat. *L'Art Pour Tous, Vol. 21.*

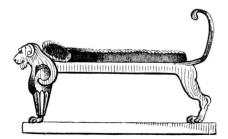

Egyptian couch. *Harper's*

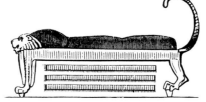

Egyptian couch. *Harper's*

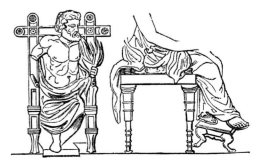

Fragments of bas relief depicting early Greek chairs. *Harper's*

Ancient continued

Portion of bas relief depicting Greek furniture.
History of Furniture

Persian royal seat. Zell's

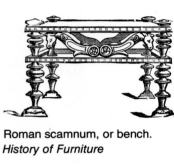

Assyrian chair.
History of Furniture

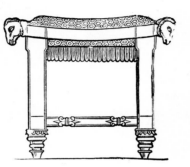

Assyrian throne.
History of Furniture

Roman scamnum, or bench.
History of Furniture

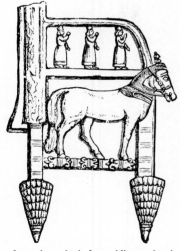

Assyrian chair from Khorsabad.
History of Furniture

Oriental throne of marble, with gilded carvings,
in the palace at Teheran. *Century Dictionary*

Roman state chair.
History of Furniture

Roman chairs. *Harper's, Vol. 46*

Throne of Queen Hatasu. *Harper's*

Ancient chair at Moor Park, England.
Leslie's

Roman white marble chair. *L'Art Pour Tous, Vol. 11*

Gothic

Because of its length, the Gothic period (1100-1453) witnessed a wide variation in the quality and kind of art it produced—from the earliest crude examples to the later luxurious and elaborate specimens. In its 350-year span, Gothic art, architecture, and decoration evolved virtually undisturbed by outside influences.

Throughout the period, French craftsmen worked primarily in stone, creating the tracery work so prevalent in Gothic churches and cathedrals. English artisans relied more on wood as a material for construction, and they surpassed their continental counterparts in the art of carving.

Gothic furniture followed closely the architectural forms then prevalent. Typical devices included the pointed arch and carved foliated ornament. Furniture for both secular and religious uses appeared in the same forms; the ecclesiastical seat was constructed of the same materials and in the same fashion as that of the master of a household.

Portability and simplicity of line are characteristic of Gothic chairs. Although stools and benches were the only common seats in use, the high-backed chair emerged as an innovation in seating. These chairs were reserved for the rich and mighty.

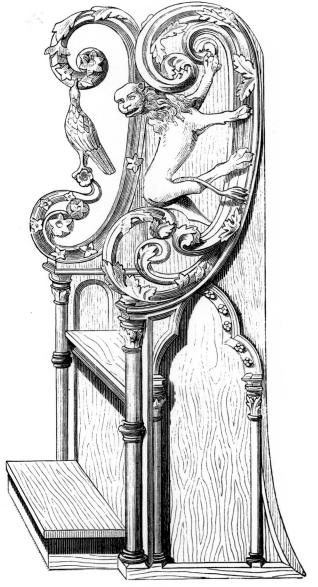

The Workshop, Vol. 8

French. *L'Art Pour Tous, Vol. 18*

Gothic continued

English carved wood canopy chair. *History of Furniture*

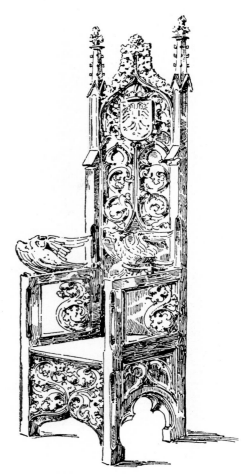

Carved oak chair. *Decorative Furniture*

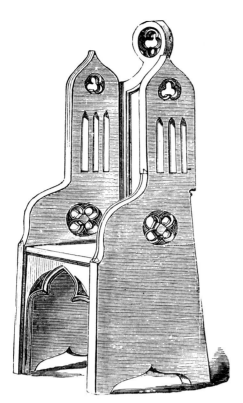

German gothic. *History of Furniture*

High-backed French gothic chair of carved oak. *History of Furniture*

English gothic. *History of Furniture*

Fifteenth century English folding stool.
History of Furniture

Gothic continued

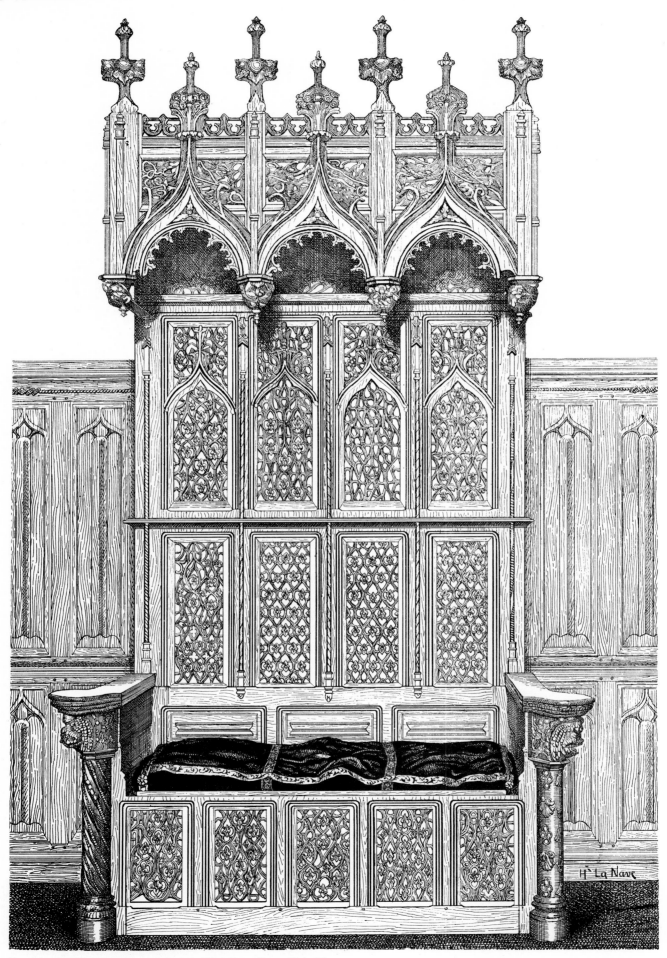

French carved oak seigneurial seat. *L'Art Pour Tous, Vol. 40*

French gothic. *L'Art Pour Tous, Vol. 41*

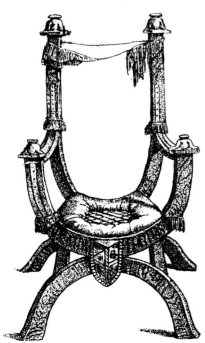

History of Furniture

German gothic.
Industry of Nations

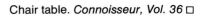

Chair table. *Connoisseur, Vol. 36* □

Tudor

Towards the end of the Gothic period, a foreign influence growing out of the Italian Renaissance took root in English furniture design. Henry VIII (1509-1547) was anxious to outdo his French contemporary, Francois I, in the elegance of his palaces. To this end, Henry imported skilled Italian and Flemish craftsmen, who brought with them the design concepts emerging in Europe. The new concepts did not obliterate the Gothic style, but rather merged with it. The synthesis of fading Gothic and rising Renaissance styles gave birth to what is known as the Tudor period of English furniture and interior design.

As early as the sixteenth century, Renaissance concepts crept into the details of English design in combination with traditional Gothic forms. In the excellent wood-carved ornaments—the Tudor rose, tracery, foliage, and arches—whispers of the growing Renaissance influence were heard.

Chairs were still relatively rare in this period. Those designed under the Tudor influence were noted for their strength and solidity. The bulbous leg was indicative of the Tudor style.

The Tudor period is often referred to as the Age of Oak. Although other native woods were sometimes used, English oak was the primary wood for both furniture and construction.

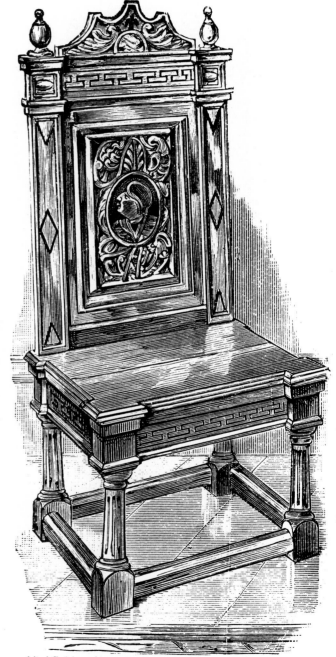

Litchfield

L'Art Pour Tous, Vol. 13

Tudor continued

L'Art Pour Tous, Vol. 31

Period Styles

L'Art Pour Tous, Vol. 41

History of Furniture

Furniture of Our Forefathers

Period Styles

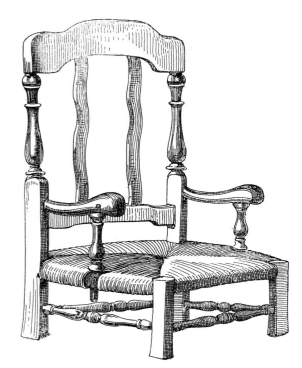

L'Art Pour Tous, Vol. 41

Jacobean

The Jacobean style, an early phase of English Renaissance design, served as a transitional school between the Elizabethan and the true Renaissance forms introduced by Inigo Jones. Jacobean embraces three distinct furniture types: Early Jacobean (1603-1649), Cromwellian (1649-1669), and Carolean (1660-1688).

Chairs of this period were severe and stout, embellished only with metal strap-work. Chairs were relatively rare possessions, and their design reflected the austere dignity of their owners. Construction depended on the mortise and tenon technique, and the joins were held together with dowels. In contrast to their continental counterparts, English cabinetmakers made no attempt to smooth or otherwise conceal chisel marks left in the wood after carving.

The typical seventeenth century English chair was an oak wainscot chair, with a cresting across the top. The spirally turned legs were low and braced, terminating in ball or bun feet. Open backs appeared with either caning, vertical balusters, or slats.

After the Restoration in 1660, chairs became common at the dining board. Throughout the Carolean period, severe straight lines softened into Flemish "S" or "C" curves, especially evident in the scrolled legs. Stretchers and top rails also became common.

From its onset, the Jacobean was largely an imported style. The Renaissance forms developed in Italy were introduced into seventeenth-century England by German and Flemish carvers. So, too, at the end of the Jacobean period, the influences operating on English furniture design were essentially foreign. English craftsmen learned from the experience of their European contemporaries.

Prior to 1660, oak had been the staple wood for construction; it was superseded by walnut when cabinetmakers realized that the popular curves, twists, and scrolls were more easily executed in walnut. Decorative devices also exhibited more refined developments. Metal strap-work and fretting, along with heavy carving, slowly gave way to inlay, turning, applied ornament, gilding, and painting. Upholstery made of brocade, velvet, and needlepoint also appeared during the Jacobean period.

Walnut chair. *Connoisseur, Vol. 15* □

Furniture of Our Forefathers

Drawing & Design

Furniture of our Forefathers

Period Styles

History of Furniture

Jacobean continued

Period Styles

Period Styles

Furniture of Our Forefathers

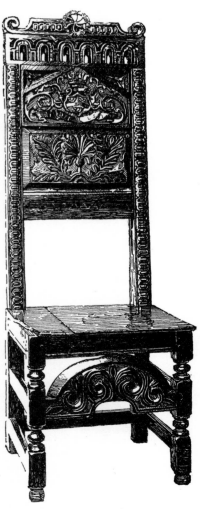

Furniture of Our Forefathers

Furniture of Our Forefathers

Furniture of Our Forefathers

Litchfield

Furniture of Our Forefathers

History of Furniture

Furniture of Our Forefathers

Furniture of Our Forefathers

Jacobean continued

History of Furniture

The master's chair. *Furniture of Our Forefathers*

Furniture of Our Forefathers

History of Furniture

Oak chair (left) surmounted by scrollwork pediment and high back walnut chair. *Furniture of Our Forefathers* □

Furniture of Our Forefathers

Spinning chair of turned wood. □

Cromwellian oak chair. *Connoisseur, Vol. 21* □

Jacobean continued

Arm chair. *Furniture of Our Forefathers* □

Period Styles

Furniture of Our Forefathers

Two arm chairs. *Furniture of Our Forefathers* □

Oak chair covered with red leather. *Litchfield* □

Jacobean continued

Furniture of Our Forefathers

Furniture of Our Forefathers □

Cromwellian oak chair. *Connoisseur, Vol. 21* □

Oak chairs. *Litchfield* □

Oak chair with high floral carved back, scroll arms, and turned legs and crossbars.
Furniture of Our Forefathers □

Renaissance

Towards the end of the fifteenth century, Europe experienced an almost universal rage for the classical in art, literature, music, and the decorative arts. Nation after nation adopted Italian art forms. Indeed, it was not until the middle of the nineteenth century that the national styles of modern European countries were revived.

In furniture design, craftsmen discarded the traditional Byzantine-Gothic mode in favor of new Renaissance forms. Chair construction was executed in walnut or chestnut, as were most other pieces of Renaissance furniture. Ornate carvings decorating the pieces were carefully finished and were of unusually fine quality. Structural elements were adorned by means of inlay.

Inlaid decoration was known as tarsia, intarsia, or certosina, terms derived from the name of the Carthusians, a religious community which produced especially fine inlay work. Ivory had been used as an inlaid material as early as 600 B.C.E. Its revival in Europe probably began in Venice at about the end of the thirteenth century. Because of the scarcity of ivory, fine bone was often used in its stead. A contrasting material—whether ivory or bone—inlaid into a dark structural material was a typically Renaissance characteristic.

Near the end of the fourteenth century, cabinetmakers began to copy marble mosaic work by making similar patterns in a variety of exotic woods. Designs ranged from simple geometric figures to entire scenes—landscapes, views of churches, figures, animals. Early Italian intarsia work picked up on this tradition, but the Renaissance craftsmen cut the decoration directly into the surface of the structural element. As the art became more refined, veneers were used, and the total effect was heightened by burning hot sand into those areas that required shading.

The character of ornament also changed during the Renaissance. In the Middle Ages, typical ornamentation depicted the saints and other religious themes, while with the Renaissance came scenes of classical mythology and allegories. Typical subjects included the elements, the seasons, the months, the cardinal virtues, and battle scenes and triumphal processions from earlier eras.

From the beginning of the sixteenth century through the middle of the seventeenth, French furniture designs reflected a rapid assimilation of Italian styles informed by French philosophy. England followed the examples of Italy and France more slowly, producing the simple and somewhat crude chair designs which became well entrenched during the reign of Elizabeth.

As the humanizing effects of the Renaissance took root, chairs became more common household objects. Their construction was solid and massive, allowing for bold carvings of honeysuckle, acanthus, bead molding and medallions. Velvet, in rich colors, was the most common fabric used for upholstery.

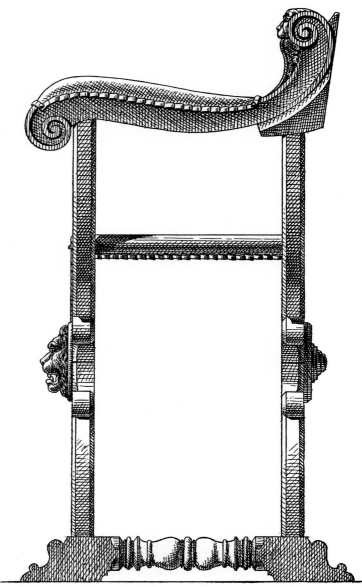

L'Art Pour Tous, Vol. 45

German. *L'Art Pour Tous, Vol. 35*

Venetian chair with carved and gilt frame,
upholstered in embroidered velvet. *Litchfield*

French carved oak arm chair. *Period Styles*

Italian. *Workshop, Vol. 8*

Renaissance continued

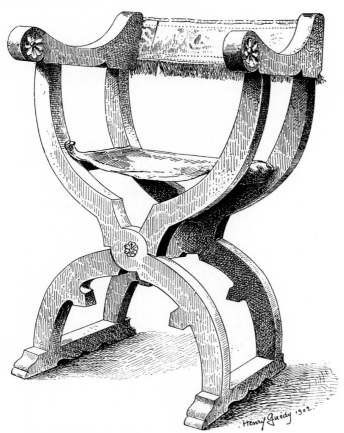

L'Art Pour Tous, Vol. 41

L'Art Pour Tous, Vol. 41

Italian. *Workshop, Vol. 8*

Italian. *History of Furniture*

Italian. *Workshop, Vol. 8*

French. *L'Art Pour Tous, Vol. 35*

Renaissance continued

French sixteenth century. *L'Art Pour Tous, Vol. 22*

German chair. *L'Art Pour Tous, Vol. 39*

Renaissance continued

Oak arm chair. *Period Styles*

History of Furniture

History of Furniture

Carved, painted, and jeweled sixteenth century Italian chairs. *L'Art Pour Tous, Vol. 6*

French stall. *L'Art Pour Tous, Vol. 6*

Sixteenth century French stall. *L'Art Pour Tous, Vol. 6*

Renaissance continued

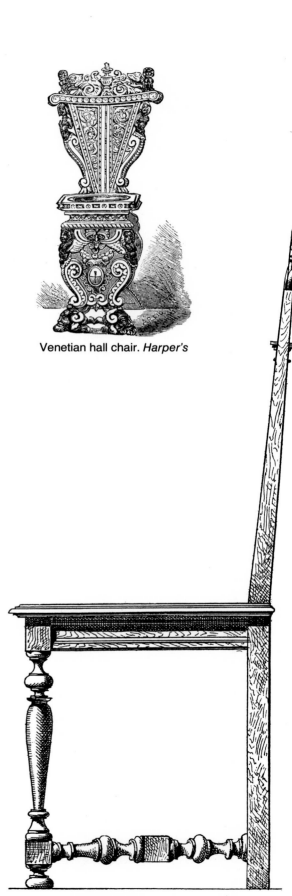

Venetian hall chair. *Harper's*

Carved wood chair. *L'Art Pour Tous, Vol. 35*

German carved wood chair. *L'Art Pour Tous, Vol. 35*

Chair covered in cuir gaufre. *Connoisseur, Vol. 10* □

Sixteenth century Spanish chair. *L'Art Pour Tous, Vol. 25*

Renaissance continued

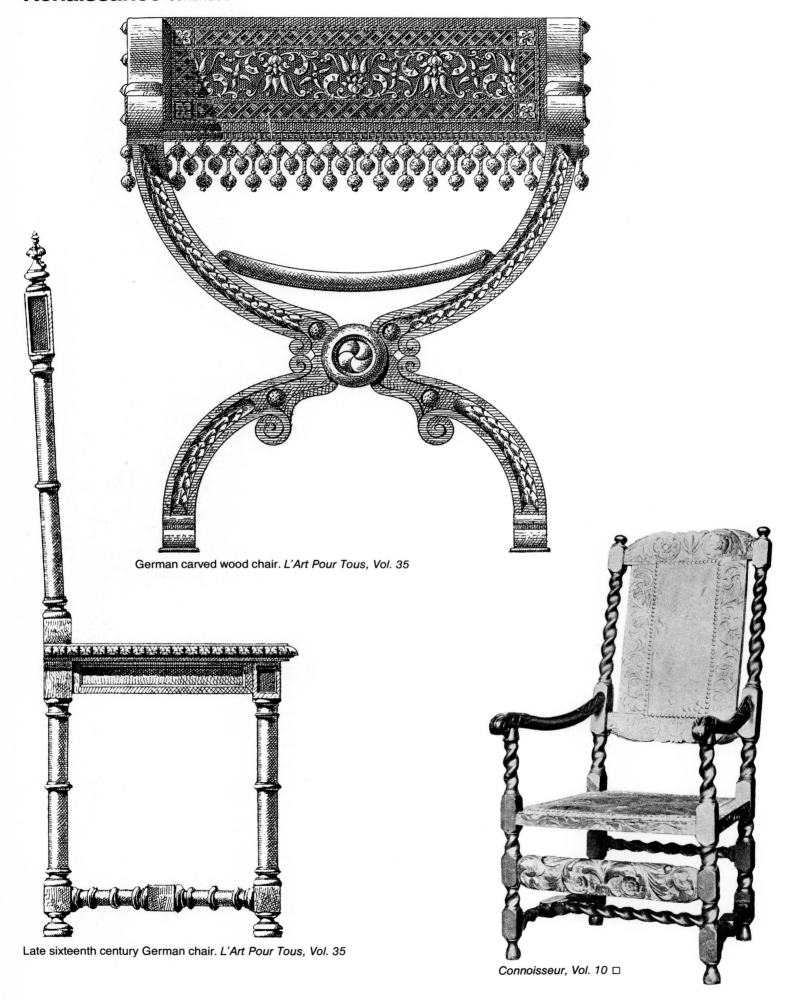

German carved wood chair. *L'Art Pour Tous, Vol. 35*

Late sixteenth century German chair. *L'Art Pour Tous, Vol. 35*

Connoisseur, Vol. 10 □

Sixteenth century Italian carved wood chair. *L'Art Pour Tous, Vol. 6*

Sixteenth century Flemish chair. *L'Art Pour Tous, Vol. 3*

Renaissance continued

Sixteenth century Italian carved wood chair. *L'Art Pour Tous, Vol. 6*

Italian folding arm chair. *Connoisseur, Vol. 10* □

Sixteenth century Flemish chair. *L'Art Pour Tous, Vol. 3*

French. *L'Art Pour Tous, Vol. 38*

Late sixteenth century German chair. *L'Art Pour Tous, Vol. 35*

Renaissance continued

Sixteenth century Portugese chair. *L'Art Pour Tous, Vol. 14*

Carved wood chair. *L'Art Pour Tous, Vol. 35*

Sixteenth century Italian folding chair. *Connoisseur, Vol. 16* □

Northern French or Flemish chair covered in tooled leather. *Connoisseur, Vol.10* □

L'Art Pour Tous, Vol. 6

Louis XIII

During the reign of Louis XIII (1610-1643), those styles of furniture design which are characteristically French came to the fore. In this period, certain preferred decorative forms evolved into a distinct style; with variations, this style was to dominate French design for roughly the next 200 years. The subsequent *Louis Quatorze, Louis Quinze,* and *Louis Seize* periods all originated in the *Louis Treize,* although variations in intensity keep these periods distinct.

Unlike preceeding chair designs, those of the *Louis Treize* style were decidely non-Italian in line and ornamentation. Trophies of arms, cartouches, festoons, bouquets, ribbons, and wreaths were lavishly employed, and gilt was freely used to obtain richness. When compared with their predecessors, *Louis Treize* chairs are flamboyant. This break with the past, however, was but a hint of the restless and extravagant detail of the rococo *(Louis Quinze)* period.

A favorite scheme for chairs of the *Louis Treize* style was the combination of crimson velvet or figured brocade with gold fringe. Since silk and velvet brocade had to be imported from Venice or from the East, imitations of these rich patterns and even cheaper substitutions were manufactured in France.

Furniture employing ebony, bone, metal, and ivory inlays became popular during the reign of Louis XIII, foreshadowing the Boulle and ormolu work of the *Louis Quatorze* style.

L'Art Pour Tous, Vol. 4

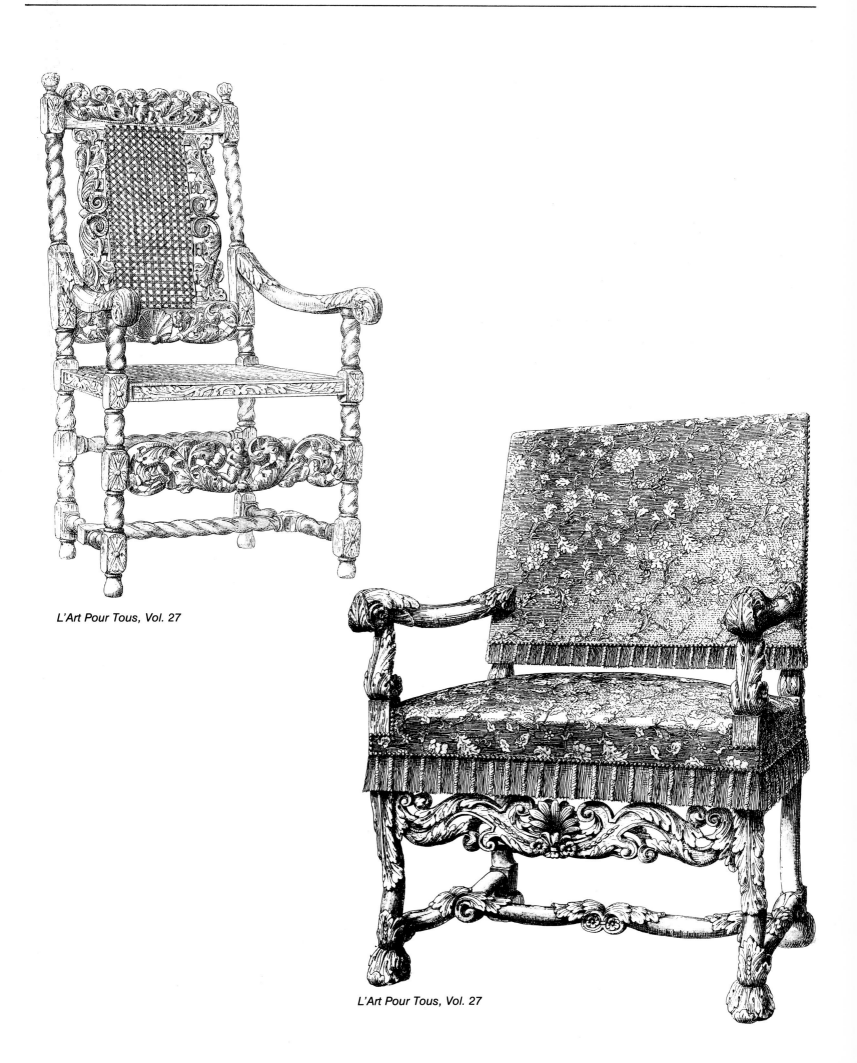

L'Art Pour Tous, Vol. 27

L'Art Pour Tous, Vol. 27

William and Mary

The reign of William and Mary (1689-1702) witnessed significant changes in furniture design which persisted through the reign of Queen Anne and well into the later part of the eighteenth century.

Especially apparent in the furniture of this period are the foreign influences; styles flourishing in France, Italy, Holland, Spain, India, and China all had some bearing on the English. By adapting the continental influences, Daniel Marot, the leading spirit in furniture design, created a solidly English school of interior decoration.

Lacquer work, marquetry, painting, gilding, and rich needlework upholstery materials were favored as means of embellishment. Simplicity of line and grace of proportion were employed to achieve comfort rather than exquisite appearance. Although the cabriole leg had begun to make its appearance during William's reign, the inverted cup leg is more characteristic of the chairs designed in the William and Mary style. Chair backs were spooned or contoured to fit the curve of the back. Brass mounts became fashionable and were applied to walnut backgrounds.

Sitting room during the William & Mary period. *Leslie's*

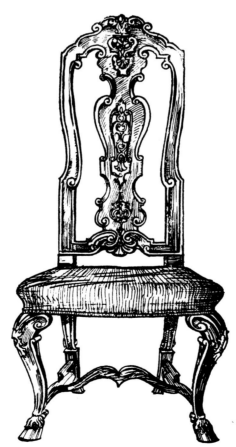

Walnut carved chair. *Period Styles*

Queen Anne

In England, the beginning of the eighteenth century witnessed the development of a new and truly English style of furniture design. Known as the Queen Anne period, this era ushered in the Golden Age of English furniture of the latter part of the eighteenth century.

Chairs produced prior to the Queen Anne period had tall backs, generally enhanced by a cane-work panel between turned or carved supports. Walnut, oak, or fruit woods were traditionally used for frame construction. Before this period, chairs were endowed with elaborately carved friezes and stretchers; the legs often exhibited the Spanish scroll toe or twisted support. Favorite means of decoration included gold, silver, and red lacquer work. The upholstery was often carried out in silk velvet.

During Queen Anne's reign, the overall design of the chair became simpler, smaller, and narrower. Carving was limited to the center splat of the chair back; occasionally, scroll work appeared at the knee or toe. Stretchers were completely eliminated from chair design. Eschewing more elaborate decoration, cabinetmakers turned to the simple shell as a decorative motif. Ultimately, the high-backed chair became nearly extinct; only hall chairs retained the design and decorative devices of previous periods.

The cabriole leg, introduced during the Queen Anne period, terminated in either a club, hoof, or spade foot. This particular characteristic of the Queen Anne period was to remain popular with furniture designers for the next forty years. The carving on the back of a Queen Anne chair echoes the shape of the chair's legs.

Another new development in chair design was the drop-in seat. This improvement allowed the veneering of the chair rail, adding to the simplicity of line. Chairs became lower, with cyma curved (vase-shaped) splats inlaid with marquetry or veneered with walnut.

Lacquer work decoration—a characteristic of Oriental furniture—also experienced a rise in popularity during the Queen Anne period. England had been importing furniture from the Orient for over a hundred years prior to the eighteenth century, but it was not until after the Restoration that the Oriental style gained popularity. The quality of Eastern cabinet work was largely inferior to that of English furniture. English craftsmen grafted Oriental forms to their traditionally fine construction techniques and obtained a superior result.

In short, Queen Anne chairs are easily identifiable by the cyma curved splat, carving confined to the splat, knee, and toe, the cabriole leg with hoof, club, or spade foot, the shell form as a decorative motif, the absence of stretchers, and the drop-in seat.

Connoisseur, Vol. 45 ☐

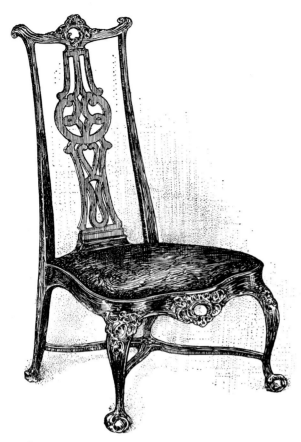

Connoissuer, Vol. 2

Walnut and gilt chair. *Connoissuer, Vol. 21* □

Connoissuer, Vol. 21 □

Walnut chair with inlaid coat of arms. *Period Styles*

Queen Anne continued

Arm chair upholstered in Spitafields silk.
History of Furniture

Tapestry covered side chair. *Period Styles*

Queen Anne arm chair. *Furniture of Our Forefathers* □

Chair upholstered in Spitalfields silk.
History of Furniture

Queen Anne side chair. *Furniture of Our Forefathers* □

Carved and upholstered arm chair. *History of Furniture*

Louis XIV

During the reign of Louis XIV (1650-1715) the artists Berain, Lebrun, and Watteau flourished. This was an era of sumptuous grandeur and extravagance—in chair design, as well as everything else.

The Palace of Versailles bears the mark of the majesty of *le Grand Monarque*. Its rich architectural ornament and interiors, with molded, gilded and painted ceilings, required furnishings of extreme ornamentation, ostentatious beyond anything that had yet appeared.

Louis XIV had good judgment in his tastes; he selected suitable artists for the creation of his palace. In 1664, the King established the Royal Academy of Painting, Architecture, and Sculpture. At this time, the celebrated Gobelins tapestry factory was founded, and it became the central workshop for the craftsmen who produced the furniture of this period.

One of the most remarkable designers of the era was Andre Charles Boulle. He originated the method of ornamenting furniture with wood and tortoise-shell veneers, and inlaying brass. This decorative technique, typical of Louis XIV furniture, bears Boulle's name. Masks, satyrs, rams' heads, scrolls of foliage, and sun motifs were typical patterns used in the Boulle method. Later in the reign of Louis XIV, as other influences were brought to bear upon the fashions and tastes of the day, styles became even more ornate. Instead of retaining the natural color of the tortoise-shell veneer, vermillion or gold leaf was placed underneath the transparent tortoise-shell. Becoming less severe, gold mounts acquired the curled endive ornament which became characteristic of the succeeding reign.

The chairs of the period reflect Louis's ardor for the magnificent and the dignified. Extensive use was made of carving and gilding, as well as lacquering, painting, inlays, and marquetry. Velvets, brocades, and tapestry from Lyons were used for upholstering the frames, which were constructed of oak, mahogany, walnut, and ebony.

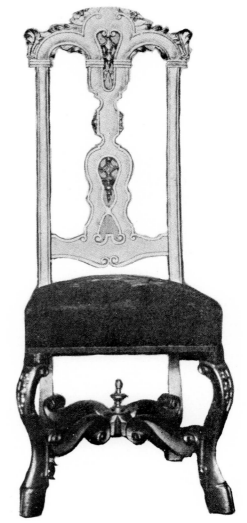

Old Furniture Book □

Old Furniture Book □

L'Art Pour Tous, Vol. 25

Louis XIV continued

L'Art Pour Tous, Vol. 25

L'Art Pour Tous, Vol. 14

L'Art Pour Tous, Vol. 14

Connoisseur, Vol. 2

Decorative Furniture

Period Styles

Louis XV

The style of Louis XV, or *Louis Quinze,* is generally known as rococo, for during the reign of this monarch (1715-1774), the extravagances which characterize the rococo style became most pronounced.

Certain elements characteristic of the rococo style were in fashion during the regime of Louis XIV, but the tastefulness and dignity of the *Quatorze* period modified and improved some of the extravagance. After Louis XV came to power, the full force of the rococo—with all its foolish extremes—arrived. Luxury, license, and frivolity were milder vices of the time. Every effort was directed toward the pursuit of gaiety, glitter, and superficiality. The boudoir became the center of activity; making it elegant and pretty preoccupied all.

The rococo is a highly artificial style. A superfluence of broken curves, abundant shell forms, and extravagant scrolls contribute to the markedly forced effect of rococo designs. The curved endive decoration, so indicative of this style, is seen everywhere in architectural ornamentation. Walls, doors, and alcoves are replete with elaborate designs in carved or molded relief: doves, wreaths, Arcadian fountains, flowing scrolls, cupids, and heads and busts of women.

Furniture accentuated the decorative treatment dictated by the rococo style. Chairs were designed on a smaller scale with more sweeping curves. The woodwork, completely or partially gilded, was upholstered in Gobelins, Beauvais, and Aubusson tapestries, or in pale silks or brocatelles. Enrichments of mother-of-pearl and marquetry became more fanciful.

Lacquerwork furnishings were fashionable during the reign of Louis XV. Chinese lacquer ware had been available to Europe ever since the Dutch had established trade routes with the Orient a century earlier. Until the mid-eighteenth century, only Chinese craftsmen had mastered the process for obtaining smooth, rich surfaces. European cabinetmakers prepared panels to be ornamented and shipped them to China to be coated with lacquer.

The delay and expense of this arrangement prompted the invention of a substitute for Oriental lacquer work. With the establishment of a French factory producing the European version of lacquerwork, the French taste for it increased. Since lacquerwork could now be done by Europeans, Oriental motifs—so firmly entrenched prior to this period—were replaced by prevailing Western designs. Produced in both monochrome and natural colors, such subjects as *Cupid Awakening Venus,* and *Nymphs and Goddesses* abounded.

With exquisite tapestries being produced in the rococo period, tapestried furniture became popular. One example was the *chase obérgère,* a new variety of arm chair with upholstered, rather than open, sides.

In general, chairs of the *Louis Quinze* style exhibited cabriole legs with strong curves. Arms, seat rails, and back frames were also curved and were elaborately carved. Mahogany, enhanced with inlay, marquetry, gilding, lacquer, and Boulle work, was used for construction of frames.

L'Art Pour Tous, Vol. 29

L'Art Pour Tous, Vol. 29

L'Art Pour Tous, Vol. 29

Louis XV continued

L'Art Pour Tous, Vol. 7

Decorative Furniture

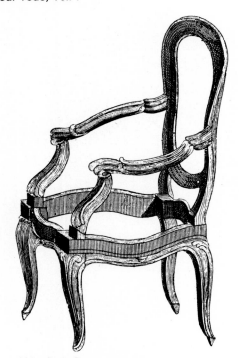

L'Art Pour Tous, Vol. 29

Decorative Furniture

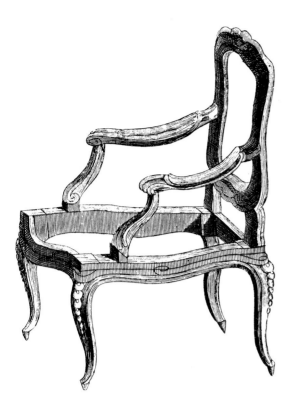

L'Art Pour Tous, Vol. 29

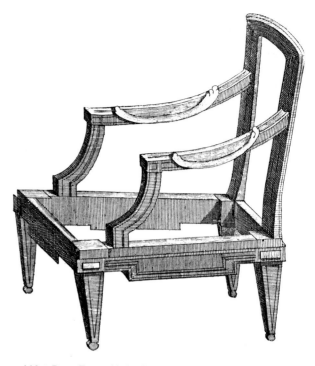

L'Art Pour Tous, Vol. 29

L'Art Pour Tous, Vol. 29

L'Art Pour Tous, Vol. 7

Chippendale

The Chippendale style includes not only the work of Thomas Chippendale, but also the work of many of his contemporaries.

During the early part of his career, Thomas Chippendale did not originate new forms; rather, he adapted previous styles. But from 1745 to 1770, his original styles dominated English furniture design. And during that era, English furniture dominated European cabinetmaking.

The most successful of Chippendale's designs were his chairs. They are distinguished by the use of mahogany for construction (a wood rarely used until the 1700s), richly carved ornamentation, and the absence of inlay decoration. The backs of Chippendale chairs were elaborately interlaced, and they had pierced splats or square tops. Graceful arms were set an angle to the back uprights. Square cabriole legs terminating in ball and claw or pad feet, lent an overall feeling of solidity.

There are four distinct types of Chippendale chairs, each type evolving through various influences. At the beginning of Chippendale's career, the two styles most popular among chair designers were Chinese and Gothic. Chippendale's translation of these two modes is evident in two types of his styles.

Chinese Chippendale chairs are symmetrical, and they employ the traditional oriental ball and claw foot, along with cane or loose cushioned seats and bamboo-like fretted backs.

Although the style proved less enduring, Gothic Chippendale gave rise to the English Gothic cluster leg, an innovation of the Chippendale school. Gothic Chippendale chairs are identified by their unique leg design; carved, angular edges; and backs designed to resemble the stained glass windows of Gothic cathedrals.

French Chippendale had its origins in the last gasps of the rococo, a prevailing style throughout eighteenth-century Europe. The rococo influence was later refined into a Chippendale adaptation of the Louis XV style. Ribbon or carved, oval backs; bowed legs; and decorative devices including gilt and elaborate carvings of scrolls, flowers, leaves, falling water, and birds are characteristic of these chairs.

The fourth, and most familiar, Chippendale type is considered the most pleasing; it is certainly the most enduring. These chairs reflect Thomas Chippendale's concern for beauty and strength. He believed that prac-

ticality of use and construction should never be subordinate to ornament. Abundant decoration, he maintained, did not necessarily result in beauty. These Chippendale chairs are remarkably solid and sturdy. They retain the roomy character of traditional Dutch furniture. The seats widen toward the front, and the backs, which flair toward the top, are invariably adorned with projecting ear-like pieces.

The name of Thomas Chippendale has become synonymous with the Golden Age of cabinetmaking in England, and his most familiar work has endured as a model of excellence.

Connoisseur, Vol. 11 □

Connoisseur, Vol. 11 □

Connoisseur, Vol. 11 □

Furniture of Our Forefathers

Furniture of Our Forefathers

Connoisseur, Vol. 20 □

Connoisseur, Vol. 3

Furniture of Our Forefathers

Furniture of Our Forefathers

Furniture of Our Forefathers

Furniture of Our Forefathers

Chippendale continued

Litchfield

Connoisseur, Vol. 12 □

*Furniture of Our
Forefathers*

*Furniture of Our
Forefathers*

Connoisseur, Vol. 11 □

Connoisseur, Vol. 6 □

Furniture of Our Forefathers

Litchfield

Furniture of Our Forefathers

Litchfield

Connoisseur, Vol. 7 □

Old Furniture Book □

Connoisseur, Vol. 8

Litchfield

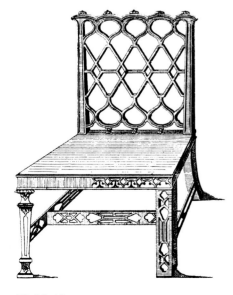

Litchfield

Furniture of Our Forefathers

Furniture of Our Forefathers

Chippendale continued

Litchfield □

Connoisseur, Vol. 6 □

Connoisseur, Vol. 6 □

Connoisseur, Vol. 6 □

Old Furniture Book □

Connoisseur, Vol. 7 □

Connoisseur, Vol. 13 □

Connoisseur, Vol. 11 □

Connoisseur, Vol. 6 □

Connoisseur, Vol. 7 □

Chippendale continued

Connoisseur, Vol. 25 □

Decorative Furniture

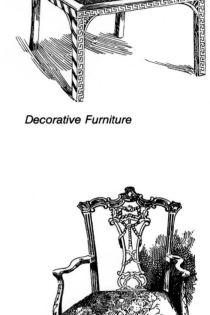

Decorative Furniture

Decorative Furniture

Connoisseur, Vol. 25 □

Connoisseur, Vol. 7 □

Connoisseur, Vol. 6 □

Connoisseur, Vol. 25 □

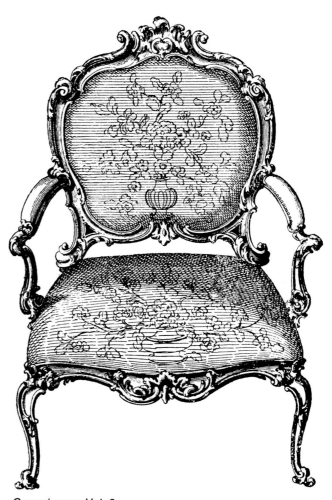

Connoisseur, Vol. 6

Connoisseur, Vol. 6 □

Connoisseur, Vol. 7 □

Connoisseur, Vol. 25 □

The Adam Brothers

Toward the end of the eighteenth century, a revolution of sorts occurred in the styles of English architecture and interior decoration. For over a hundred years prior to this time, there had been an unbroken sequence of fine design carried on in stages of consistent growth. Breaking with this pattern, Robert and James Adam turned their attention to classical Greece and Rome. By reintroducing the ancient forms of design into contemporary styles, the brothers achieved the distinctive Adam style of architecture and interior design.

Furniture designs were not just inspired by classical forms; the furniture had to be suitable for use in Greek or Roman style rooms, which the Adam brothers, as architects, also built. Of course, many pieces of furniture necessary for furnishing an eighteenth-century house had no prototype in classical Greece or Rome. But the Adam brothers skillfully adapted ancient forms to modern needs and tastes.

Perhaps the most successful synthesis of ancient form and contemporary need was the Adam chair. Eliminating the ubiquitous Grecian curve, the Adam brothers instead used small, straight, tapering legs. The legs were often fluted (a modern construction technique), and cut concavely or reeded, terminating in a spade foot.

The chair backs were oval with solid wood frames. Satinwood was used extensively for inlay work or even for total construction. The Adam brothers favored such decorative devices as gilding, plaques and cameo insets, and paintings of classical scenes. Delicate, low relief carvings of sphinxes, wreaths, flower garlands, urns, and fans were also characteristic.

No detail was considered too insignificant to warrant attention. The Adam brothers designed not only the frames and structural elements of their chairs, but they also became involved in choosing the patterns used for upholstery. Wool plush, heavy silk, and French brocade were among the favored textiles.

The Adam chair was part of a total concept of interior design. The classical elements used in furniture were echoed in the carpets, ceiling, wall decorations—indeed, in every item of furnishing down to the fire irons. Under the influence of the Adam brothers, buildings, rooms, and furniture all complimented each other.

Arm chair, covered in figured velvet. *Litchfield* □

Connoisseur, Vol. 45 □

Connoisseur, Vol. 25 □

Connoisseur, Vol. 9 □

Furniture of Our Forefathers

Connoisseur, Vol. 29 □

Furniture of Our Forefathers

Furniture of Our Forefathers

Connoisseur, Vol. 9 □

Louis XVI

Under the regime of Louis XVI (1774-1793), the extravagance of the rococo gave way to a more pure and simple style. Broken scrolls were replaced by straight lines. In the ornamental facades of public buildings, curves and arches were introduced, and columns and pillars reappeared. Interior decoration necessarily followed suit.

Adopted as a reaction to the preceeding style, this revival of classical forms was encouraged by discoveries of ancient treasures in Herculaneum and Pompeii. Drawings and reproductions from frescoes found in these old Italian cities served as models for the cabinetmakers of the day.

The influence of ancient forms can be seen in the decorative devices used in chairs of the *Louis Seize* period. A favorite scheme combined carved and gilt wood frames with the pictorial tapestries of Beauvais. Represented in these fabrics were scenes of pastoral life: genteel shepherdesses, idealized farm laborers, and delicate milkmaids.

Boulle and ormolu work underwent a revival, but here again, the rococo twists and curls gave way to more sober details. Ornaments were restricted to a few severe festoons, classic wreaths, or trellis work of squares or diamonds, emphasized by floral bosses or studs.

Chair design of this period emphasized vertical and horizontal lines. Legs were straight, tapered, and fluted. Mahogany, satinwood, and a variety of ornamental woods were most often used for construction.

The *Louis Seize* period, though less grand than the *Louis Quatorze*, produced chairs that were consistently beautiful. *Louis Seize* designers discarded the feverish, fantastic rococo in favor of the more controlled, more chaste classical modes.

History of Furniture

Period Styles

Decorative Furniture

Decorative Furniture

L'Art Pour Tous, Vol. 30

Louis XVI continued

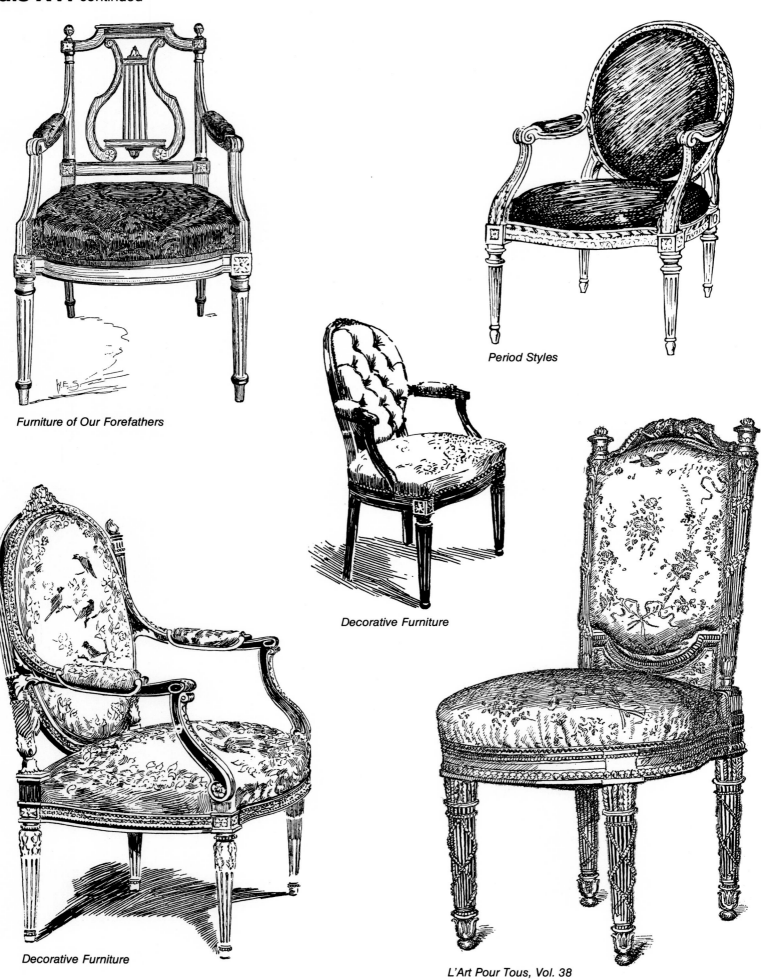

Furniture of Our Forefathers

Period Styles

Decorative Furniture

Decorative Furniture

Workshop, Vol. 5

Decorative Furniture

L'Art Pour Tous, Vol. 40

Louis XVI continued

L'Art Pour Tous, Vol. 31

L'Art Pour Tous, Vol. 38

Litchfield

Litchfield

Litchfield

Old Furniture Book □

Decorative Furniture

Louis XVI continued

Chair of white enameled wood upholstered with Beauvais tapestry. *Litchfield* □

Carved and gilt **wood** chairs covered with Beauvais tapestry. *Connoisseur, Vol. 2*

Arm chair of carved, painted and gilt wood, with Beauvais tapestry seat, back, and arm pieces. *L'Art Pour Tous, Vol. 28*

Sheraton

Along with Thomas Chippendale, Thomas Sheraton is one of the most famous English furniture designers and cabinetmakers.

Much of Sheraton's fame rests on a remarkable series of books Sheraton published at the end of his career. The first of these volumes, published in 1971, was entitled *The Cabinetmaker and Upholsterer's Drawing Book*.

Sheraton's chair designs were exceedingly varied, but all of his work is distinguished by grace of line, refinement of decoration, and logical construction. Structural portions of his chairs are seldom hidden by tortuous curves; supports and joints are frankly designed for their purpose. Applied decoration never dominates utility.

The fluted legs of the typical Sheraton chair are slender and straight, tapering toward the foot. The carved decoration is done in low relief, and most often consists of rosettes, ribbons, acanthi, and small bell flowers.

Satinwood inlay is a characteristic decorative device of the Sheraton chair. The patterns consist of motives of ovals or fan shapes, circles with radiating lines, leaf and festoon forms.

Although no one contests the grace and pleasing proportions evident in Sheraton's designs, the student of furniture acknowledges the tremendous influence of both Hepplewhite and Adam on Sheraton's work. Some critics have suggested that Sheraton actually collaborated with Adam for several years.

But Sheraton's slender forms and sweeping curves were products of his own inspiration. Moreover, his extensive use of satinwood provides a unique and distinguishing characteristic that differentiates his work from those of the cabinetmakers preceeding him.

Furniture of Our Forefathers

History of Furniture

Furniture of Our Forefathers

History of Furniture

Drawing room chair. *Litchfield*

Connoisseur, Vol. 13 □

Decorative Furniture

Connoisseur, Vol. 2

Decorative Furniture

Sheraton continued

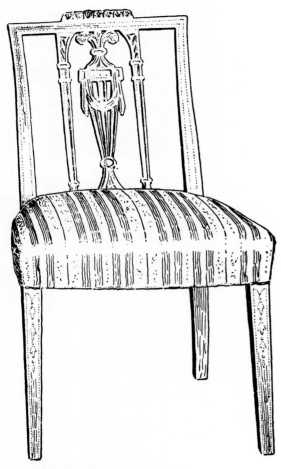

Furniture of Our Forefathers

Furniture of Our Forefathers

Connoisseur, Vol. 12 □

Furniture of Our Forefathers

Period Styles

Period Styles

Furniture of Our Forefathers

Furniture of Our Forefathers

Connoisseur, Vol. 10 □

Furniture of Our Forefathers

Furniture of Our Forefathers

Sheraton continued

Old Furniture Book □

Furniture of Our Forefathers

Connoisseur, Vol. 3

Windsor chair designed by Sheraton. *Old Furniture Book* □

Sheraton arm chair. *Furniture of Our Forefathers*

Litchfield

Furniture of Our Forefathers □

Hepplewhite

The term "Hepplewhite" refers to a style of furniture rather than to the work of any one man. Hepplewhite chairs are distinguished by their delicacy and grace; the hallmark of this particular style is lightness. These are extremely pretty chairs. Unlike those designed by Chippendale, who sought solidity and careful construction, Hepplewhite chairs, with their light and delicate appearance, were accused of fragility and faulty construction.

Analyses have shown that the furniture was well constructed and certainly bears the weight of a man. Up to this time, the splat always joined the seat of a chair, making it stronger. Instead of bringing the splat down to the seat, George Hepplewhite designed it to curve and join the side rails three or four inches above the seat.

Hepplewhite chairs are easily recognizable by their peculiar backs. These were often ornamented with festooned heads of wheat, pointed fern leaves, and the feathers identified with the coat of arms of the Prince of Wales (supposedly, George IV, while he held the title of Prince of Wales, sponsored A. Hepplewhite & Company).

Distinctive ornament, as well as lightness of design, identifies the Hepplewhite chair from others which were designed and constructed during this same period. One of George Hepplewhite's favorite decorative devices was the use of japanned work or laquer. Most frequently, he employed patterns of fruits and flowers on a black background. Many Hepplewhite chairs are painted with wreaths and festoons, with amorini and musical instruments, and with floral motifs. Unfortunately, these impermanent decorations wore off with comparatively little use.

Another favorite element evident in Hepplewhite's designs is the circle (or a portion of it). His chair backs are nearly always round or oval. These backs often contain a central ornament of Prince of Wales feathers or sheaves of drooping wheat.

Inlay work of exotic woods is another characteristic feature of Hepplewhite chairs. Tulip, rose, snake, and panella woods were used for inlay and marquetry. These techniques often appear in the husk pattern which resembles the spreading husks of ripe oats. The elements of the chair itself were designed in a distinctive manner. Hepplewhite chair legs were most often slender and tapering, and terminated in a splade foot. Inlay work, commonly used in the design of Hepplewhite chair legs,

ran down approximately half the length of the leg. Although George Hepplewhite favored satinwood for construction, ebony and holly were used as well.

Many modern chairs were inspired by the designs of this master cabinetmaker. The winged easy chair is most certainly attributable to Hepplewhite. In its day, it was probably the most comfortable chair in general use.

According to knowledgeable sources, Hepplewhite furniture ranged from elegant and delicate to unimaginative and pedestrian. This diversity may be explained by the fact that Hepplewhite furniture was the creation of a school of cabinetmakers who took their lead from George Hepplewhite. Some of these craftsmen produced work of superior and distinctive design, while others were not so imaginative nor able.

Connoisseur, Vol. 40 □

Connoisseur, Vol. 40 □

Furniture of Our Forefathers

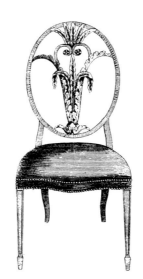

Litchfield

Litchfield

Furniture of Our Forefathers

Decorative Furniture

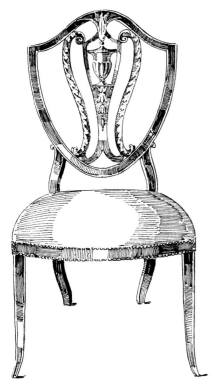

Litchfield

Connoisseur, Vol. 1

Hepplewhite continued

Connoisseur, Vol. 14 □

Litchfield

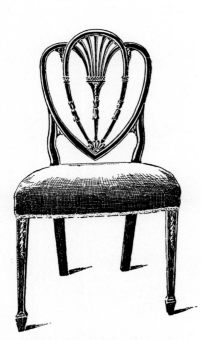

Furniture of Our Forefathers

Connoisseur, Vol. 10 □

Connoisseur, Vol. 11 □

Connoisseur, Vol. 10 □

Connoisseur, Vol. 10 □

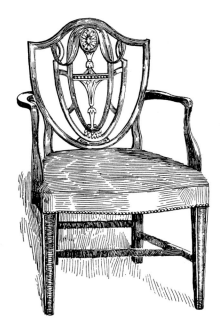

Decorative Furniture

Empire

Following the French Revolution, a period of despotic rule under Napoleon gave rise to the somewhat stiff and stilted Empire style of decoration. France's Emperor dictated fashion as well as social and governmental policy, and his love for Roman grandeur inspired the new rage for classicism in the decorative arts.

Housed in the Vatican were marble, stone, and bronze fragments from ancient chairs; these provided the inspiration for much of the furniture of the Empire style. In their attempt to reproduce Greek, Roman, and sometimes Egyptian forms, cabinetmakers employed the classical tripod as their chief support. Empire chairs recall the straight and uncluttered lines associated with classical design.

The Empire style harkened back to the classical age in decorative, as well as structural, devices. Indeed, much of the visual interest in Empire chairs is generated by the sharp contrast between the stark frames and the gilt and chased ormolu mountings. Invariably, the mounts represented ancient themes: antique Roman fasces, trophies of lances surmounted by the Phrygian cap of liberty, winged figures emblematic of freedom, and antique heads of helmeted warriors arranged like cameo medallions. When applied to the rich-toned mahogany of the frame, the mountings were particularly striking. In addition, vivid blue, green, purple, and red upholstery was used extensively.

Though essentially a French movement, the Empire style spread to England, where it gave rise to the Early Victorian style. Students maintain, however, that the English retained only the least desirable elements of the Empire school.

History of Furniture □

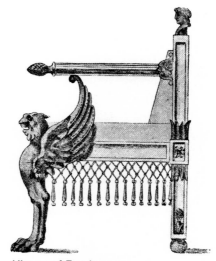

History of Furniture □

History of Furniture

Decorative Furniture

Connoisseur, Vol. 15 □

Decorative Furniture

Decorative Furniture

Period Styles

American

Although in its early history the United States produced some native styles of furniture design, most furniture was based on English and European designs. The styles of American furniture fall into four distinct categories: Colonial (1620-1775), Revolutionary (1775-1789), Federalist (1789-1812), and Empire (1812-1850).

The plain, rugged colonial furniture of the seventeenth century was homemade. The designs were those with which the settlers were familiar—Elizabethan and Jacobean.

Although design characteristics were borrowed from the mother country, colonial furniture did have distinctive qualities of its own. Oak, pine, maple, cherry, and other native woods were used for construction. Chair elements were fitted together either by the mortise and tenon technique or by dovetailing. Since screws were unavailable and glue was seldom used in building the frame, square wooden pins held the pieces firm. The methods of decoration were simple, including chamfering, molding, turning, carving, and painting.

The Carver chair is an example of the English Jacobean style translated into the American idiom. It was constructed entirely of turned fittings joined horizontally and vertically. John Carver, first governor of the Plymouth Colony, is said to have owned a chair of this design—hence, its name. The Carver chair was adapted for use as a side chair by removing the arms. The well-known Brewster chair is an elaboration of this design.

Originating in colonial times, the slat-backed chair was long a staple of American furnishing. Usually constructed of native hardwoods, the chair had two to six graduated slats running horizontally across its back; it could be built with or without arms. The seats of slat-back chairs were made of rush or splint. Popular in the seventeenth century, this design continued to be used throughout the eighteenth century and on into the nineteenth century, when it was adapted by the Shakers.

The Windsor chair, probably of English peasant origin, also had its American version. While the American Windsor contained only shaved upright spindles, its English counterpart was often produced with cabriole legs. The hoop-back, low-back, fan-back, and comb-back were all familiar types of American Windsor chairs. Commonly, the legs and backs of these chairs were made of hickory, ash, beech, or maple, while soft woods (such as pine) were used for the seats; construction from a single type of wood was rare.

A purely American adaptation of the Windsor chair was the writing arm chair, typified by the addition of a large, pear-shaped desk arm often containing a drawer. Such a wide variety of these chairs exist, that it is evident that the particular tastes and purposes of the customer dictated the construction of each chair.

The eighteenth century, which includes both the Revolutionary and Federalist periods of American furniture, witnessed a significant European influence on interior design, but the furniture produced in these periods was distinctly American in its sturdy construction and simple lines.

The Martha Washington chair is an adaptation of Hepplewhite's design. Produced in the late eighteenth century, it had a high, canted, upholstered back and tapered, square legs. Not all Martha Washington chairs were manufactured with arms, but if there were arms, they were rarely upholstered.

American craftsmen working at the time of the Revolutionary War made a unique contribution: the rocking chair. The Boston rocker, dubbed "the most popular chair ever made," is an adaptation of the Windsor chair set on rockers. It was usually designed with arms, a rounded top, and a rolling seat.

By the middle of the eighteenth century, the quality of American furniture rivaled that produced in England. Duncan Phyfe, a notable American designer of this period, combined the finer elements of English Georgian design with the simplicity of eighteenth century French furniture.

Phyfe's work, characteristic of the Empire period, was built for domestic use. His chairs were strong, finely finished, and classic in proportion. The repetition of the lyre form, the curule leg, classic curves, and Greek and Roman decorative devices are characteristic of this style. Phyfe worked almost exclusively in mahogany.

The so-called Fancy chair, an outgrowth of Phyfe and Sheraton designs, was delicate in form and extremely lightweight. Usually constructed of soft pine, these chairs were painted black and then decorated with gold and flower motifs. The seats were made of cane or rush. During the early part of the nineteenth century, the Fancy chair was manufactured in large quantities, and became as staple of American furnishing.

Furniture of Our Forefathers

Furniture of Our Forefathers

Furniture of Our Forefathers

Furniture of Our Forefathers

Furniture of Our Forefathers

Furniture of Our Forefathers

Furniture of Our Forefathers

American continued

Furniture of Our Forefathers

Furniture of Our Forefathers

Furniture of Our Forefathers

Furniture of Our Forefathers

Furniture of Our Forefathers

Furniture of Our Forefathers

Furniture of Our Forefathers

Furniture of Our Forefathers

Furniture of Our Forefathers

Furniture of Our Forefathers

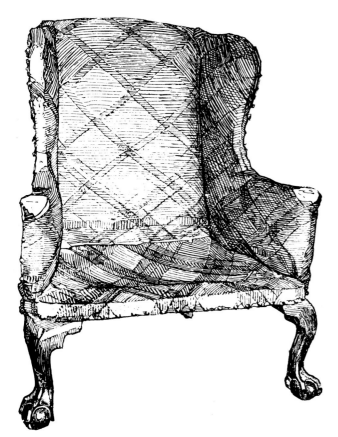

Furniture of Our Forefathers

Furniture of Our Forefathers

Furniture of Our Forefathers

American continued

Carved rosewood chair
upholstered in silk brocade.
Furniture of Our Forefathers □

Arm chair from the Van
Rensselaer Manor House,
Albany, New York. *Furniture of
Our Forefathers*

Furniture of Our Forefathers

Child's hardwood
rocker with painted
ornaments.
*Montgomery Ward
Catalog*

Child's reed rocking
chair. *Montgomery
Ward Catalog*

Hardwood dining
chair with double
bent top rail and
spindle back.
*Montgomery Ward
Catalog*

Nineteenth century
dining room chair
with carved top rail
and cane seat.
*Montgomery Ward
Catalog*

Nineteenth century birch framed spring rocker upholstered in velour. *Sears Catalog*

Side chair upholstered in Morocco leather with black-stained pear wood frame. *Workshop, Vol. 2*

Natural reed reception hall or corner chair. *Montgomery Ward Catalog*

Birch wood side chair with camel-back rail and pierced splat. *Sears Catalog*

Wheel-back windsor chair. *Connoissuer, Vol. 45* □

American continued

Lady's reed rocker with maple base. *Montgomery Ward Catalog*

Ornamental wicker rocker with white maple base. *Montgomery Ward Catalog*

Lady's wicker rocking chair. *Montgomery Ward Catalog*

Nineteenth century veranda rocker with hardwood posts and reed seat and back. *Montgomery Ward Catalog*

Nineteenth century lady's reed rocker. *Montgomery Ward Catalog*

Nineteenth century reed rocker. *Montgomery Ward Catalog*

Lady's braided reed rocker. *Montgomery Ward Catalog*

Nineteenth century lady's hardwood rocker. *Montgomery Ward Catalog*

Tufted reading chair with solid oak frame and carved seat rail. *Sears Catalog*

Lady's rocker of natural reed. *Montgomery Ward Catalog*

Gentleman's reeded arm rocker. *Montgomery Ward Catalog*

Carved mahogany arm chair with pierced back. *Sears Catalog*

Morris chair of solid oak with adjustable back and reversible cushions. *Sears Catalog*

World's Fair rolling invalid chair of reed, with ball bearing and rubber cushioned wheels. *Montgomery Ward Catalog*

Solid oak gentleman's rocker with carved top rail. *Montgomery Ward Catalog*

Solid oak dining room chair with cane seat. *Montgomery Ward Catalog*

High-backed painted lawn chair. *Montgomery Ward Catalog*

Richly carved birch parlor chair. *Sears Catalog*

Solid oak Morris chair with adjustable back and loose cushioned seat. *Sears Catalog*

Nineteenth century mahogany parlor chair in the Roman style. *Sears Catalog*

Solid oak dining room chair with spindle back and carved top rail. *Montgomery Ward Catalog*

Gentleman's high-backed rocker with flat roll seat. *Montgomery Ward Catalog*

Nineteenth century wicker rocking chair. *Montgomery Ward Catalog*

Nineteenth century reed rocker with braided border. *Montgomery Ward Catalog*

Nineteenth century spring rocker. *Sears Catalog*

Mahogany side chair with upholstered seat and shield back. *Furniture of Our Forefathers*

Hardwood dining chair with spindle back and pierced top rail. *Montgomery Ward Catalog*

Ornamental lady's reed rocker. *Montgomery Ward Catalog*

Nineteenth century birch frame arm chair with pierced splat. *Sears Catalog*

Gentleman's large reed rocking chair. *Montgomery Ward Catalog*

Hardwood dining chair with spindle back and top rail. *Montgomery Ward Catalog*

Nineteenth century Turkish parlor occasional chair with tufted headrest. *Sears Catalog*

American continued

Furniture of Our Forefathers

Furniture of Our Forefathers

Furniture of Our Forefathers

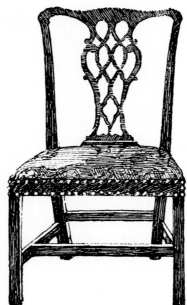

Furniture of Our Forefathers

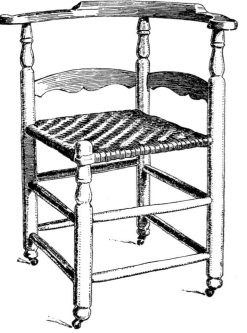

Furniture of Our Forefathers

Connoisseur, Vol. 10

James Fenimore Cooper armchair with drawer for writing materials (reproduction circa 1927). *Hart* □

Furniture of Our Forefathers

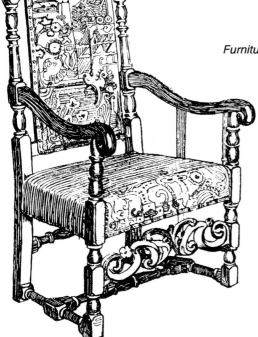

Furniture of Our Forefathers

Furniture of Our Forefathers

Industry of Nations

American continued

Nineteenth century
American chair.
Harper's, Vol. 53

Buckeye arm chair of
rock elm with cane
seat. *Montgomery
Ward Catalog*

Walnut arm chair with cabriole
legs. *Furniture of Our Forefathers*

Carved oak hall chair. *Furniture
of Our Forefathers*

Furniture of Our Forefathers

Washington's secretary and chair.
Harper's, Vol. 18

Walnut side chair. *Furniture of
Our Forefathers*

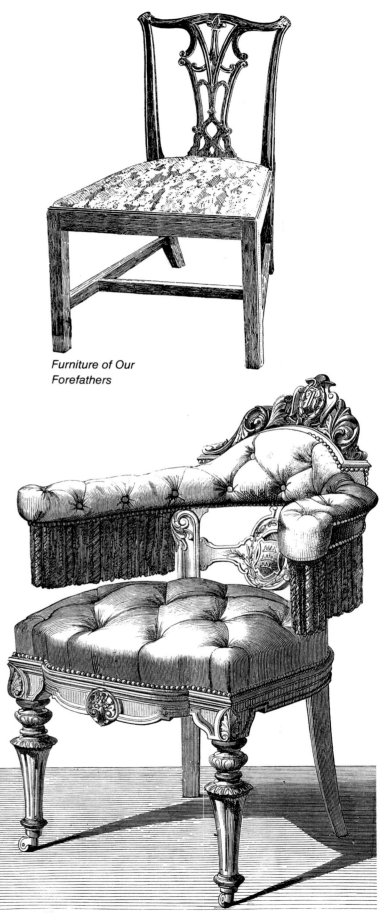

Furniture of Our
Forefathers

Turned chair with straight stretchers and upholstered in leather.
Old Furniture Book □

Easy chair of mahogany, covered
with leather.
Century Magazine □

Stuffed arm chair, upholstered in
Morocco leather with
black-stained pear wood frame.
Workshop, Vol. 2

American continued

Furniture of Our Forefathers

Bent back hardwood dining chair with scoop seat. *Montgomery Ward Catalog*

Folding hammock garden chair with hardwood frame and canvas sling seat. *Montgomery Ward Catalog*

Turned and carved oak arm chair. *Old Furniture Book* □

Fancy chair with rush seat and landscape painting adorning top rail. *Furniture of Our Forefathers*

Carved, solid mahogany dining room arm chair with leather upholstered seat and back. *Montgomery Ward Catalog*

Side chair from the Van Rensselaer Manor House, Albany, New York. *Furniture of Our Forefathers*

Hardwood arm chair with carved top rail and upholstered back and seat. *Sears Catalog*

Nineteenth century swivel chair with spring mechanism. *Montgomery Ward Catalog*

Cane seated side chair with carved top rail. *Montgomery Ward Catalog*

Furniture of Our Forefathers

Nineteenth century arm and side chair. *Workshop, Vol. 2*

American continued

Furniture of Our Forefathers

Rush-bottomed
chairs. *Old Furniture
Book* □

Furniture of Our Forefathers

Century Magazine

Nineteenth century Turkish parlor
arm chair. *Sears Catalog*

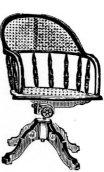

Office chair with half
cane seat and screw
and spring
mechanism.
*Montgomery Ward
Catalog*

Maclean patent swing
rocker of carved oak with
leather cobbler seat. *Sears
Catalog*

Nineteenth century
American chair.
Harper's, Vol. 53

Ornamental wicker
occasional chair.
*Montgomery Ward
Catalog*

Child's high chair
with wood seat and
table piece.
*Montgomery Ward
Catalog*

Nineteenth century Morris chair with adjustable back. *Sears Catalog*

Folding camp chair with slat seat and back. *Montgomery Ward Catalog*

High-backed lady's wicker rocking chair. *Montgomery Ward Catalog*

Furniture of Our Forefathers □

Chair of dried elm unfolds into a step ladder. *Montgomery Ward Catalog*

Nineteenth century hardwood high chair. *Montgomery Ward Catalog*

Hardwood occasional chair with carved top rail. *Sears Catalog*

English

In England, as in Europe, chairs were scarce during the first half of the sixteenth century. Only the master and mistress of a household sat in chairs; less illustrious people used settles and benches. Chairs were also very plain, the only means of decoration being loose cushions, and perhaps, minimal carving.

With the reign of Queen Elizabeth (1558-1603), wood carving became more ambitious. Presumably, English craftsmen acquired much of their skill from the proficient Flemish carvers who had settled in England. In comparison with contemporary carving of other nations, the Elizabethan style was far more grotesque, exhibiting griffins, goblins, and deformed animals.

During the reign of Charles II (1630-1685), the use of chairs as common household articles grew rapidly. In this period (the Jacobean), the English cabinetmaker's craft became more refined. The importation of scarce foreign woods encouraged the development of inlay work, which until Elizabeth's time had been crude. Marquetry in Italy, France, Holland, Germany, and Spain had already attained a high degree of excellence.

The development of English furniture progressed through the William and Mary, the Queen Anne, and the Georgian periods, each influenced by prevailing European styles. From the *Louis Quatorze* period, England inherited a strong partiality for gilt furniture constructed with similar lines as the French, but the English varieties were heavy and clumsy, lacking the spirit and grace of the French originals.

For approximately thirty years after the end of Queen Anne's reign, English furniture exhibited no radical changes; elaborating upon already established conventions was the order of the day. Thus, out of the Queen Anne style arose the Decorated Queen Anne design, the Lion design, the Satyr-mask design, and the Cabochon-and-leaf design. This progression, based on the simple, elegant lines of the Queen Anne concept, culminated in the Golden Age of English furniture, which coincided with Chippendale's popularity.

Chippendale, Hepplewhite, Sheraton, and the Adam brothers dominated English furniture design during the latter half of the eighteenth century. Although these master craftsmen worked during the reigns of the Georges, their unique designs are not considered part of the undistinguished Georgian school, which was characterized by massive mahogany, oak, and walnut furnishings.

In the early nineteenth century, Napoleon dictated the institution of the Empire style in France. When adopted by the English, this neo-classic style foundered, becoming what many consider the tasteless Victorian style.

Decorative Furniture

The Gladstonbury chair. *Harper's*

Industry of Nations

The Dunmow chair. *Harper's*

English continued

Drawing room chair. *Harper's*

Oak revolving and tilting office chair with solid wood seat. *Spiers & Pond's Catalog*

Decorative Furniture

Heraldic chair. *Industry of Nations*

Industry of Nations

London Bridge chair. *Connoisseur, Vol. 13* □

Industry of Nations

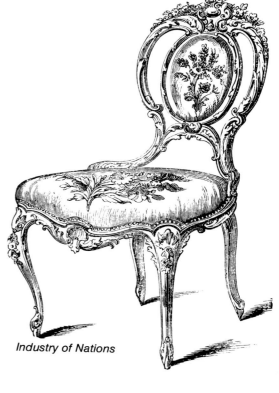

Industry of Nations

Industry of Nations

Industry of Nations

Drawing room chair. *Harper's*

English continued

Litchfield

Period Styles

Office chair with cane seat. *Spier's & Pond's Catalog*

Industry of Nations

Bentwood side chair with cane seat. *Spiers & Pond's Catalog*

Revolving chair upholstered in leather. *Spiers & Pond's Catalog*

Revolving chair with wooden seat. *Spiers & Pond's Catalog*

Litchfield □

Wing-backed easy chair upholstered in tapestry. *Spiers & Pond's Catalog*

Nineteenth century inlaid mahogany corner chair. *Spiers & Pond's Catalog*

L'Art Pour Tous, Vol. 30

Wood revolving office chair on casters. *Spiers & Pond's Catalog*

Inlaid mahogany arm chair with silk tapestry seat. *Spiers & Pond's Catalog*

Benwood wide chair with straight side pieces, top rail, and caned seat. *Spiers & Pond's Catalog*

English continued

Connoisseur, Vol. 36 □

Mahogany inlaid corner chair with silk upholstery seat. *Spiers & Pond's Catalog*

Carved, upholstered chair. *Industry of Nations*

Inlaid mahogany armchair with silk tapestry seat. *Spiers & Pond's Catalog*

Lounge chair with loose seat cushion upholstered in tapestry. *Spiers & Pond's Catalog*

Carved wood, upholstered chair. *Industry of Nations*

Semi-circular office chair upholstered in leather. *Spiers & Pond's Catalog*

L'Art Pour Tous, Vol. 22

Ebony chair. *Harper's*

Oak revolving and tilting office chair with leather upholstered seat. *Spiers & Pond's Catalog*

Nineteenth century tapestry upholstered arm chair. *Spiers & Pond's Catalog*

English continued

Carved and gilt frame chair, upholstered in silk and embroidered with the royal coat of arms of the Prince of Wales. *History of Furniture*

Connoisseur, Vol. 21 □

Gentleman's bentwood rocker with caned seat and back. *Spiers & Pond's Catalog*

Mahogany occasional chair. *Spiers & Pond's Catalog*

Birch chair upholstered in Utrecht velvet. *Spiers & Pond's Catalog*

Arm chair with inlaid mahogany frame and tapestry arms, seat, and back. *Spiers & Pond's Catalog*

Lounge chair with double spring seat, stuffed with horsehair and covered in silk tapestry. *Spiers & Pond's Catalog*

Nineteenth century
mahogany arm chair.
Spiers & Pond's Catalog

Oak revolving and tilting
chair with perforated
veneer seat. *Spiers &
Pond's Catalog*

Oak Yorkshire chair. *Connoisseur, Vol. 21* □

Nineteenth century carved
mahogany side chair with
silk brocade seat. *Spiers &
Pond's Catalog*

Carved mahogany arm
chair covered in silk
brocade. *Spiers & Pond's
Catalog*

French

France, especially during the Louis periods, was a leading influence on the development of furniture design. France quickly picked up the essence of the Renaissance from its neighbor, Italy. By incorporating the Renaissance spirit into their chairs, French cabinetmakers helped spread the new concepts throughout Europe.

In contrast to the grandeur that marked all the Louis periods was the homely style of French provincial chairs. French provincial developed outside the cultural centers of the nation, and while both styles emerged simultaneously, each had little influence on the other.

Little of note appeared in French furniture design before the emergence of Louis XIII as king. It is for this reason that the spectacular rise of the Louis styles as the acme of French furniture design is all the more incredible. The *Louis Quatorze* and *Louis Quinze* periods were especially prolific in chair construction. One cannot overestimate the enormous influence of these schools on the cabinetmakers of England and the continent. Chippendale and Sheraton produced some of the best known English translations of these French designs.

As chair design moved into the modern period, national design concepts—of France as well as other countries—virtually ceased, because improved transportation and communication have internationalized the influences on all furniture design.

Furniture of Our Forefathers

Decorative Furniture

Industry of Nations

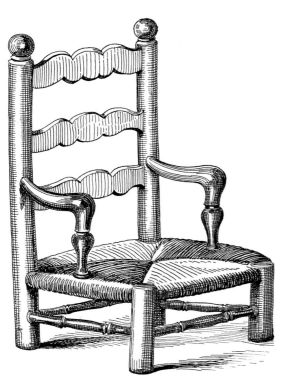

L'Art Pour Tous, Vol. 21

Furniture of Our Forefathers

French continued

L'Art Pour Tous, Vol. 40

Side and arm chair in beech gilt with silk upholstery designed in Paris during the late nineteenth century. *Workshop, Vol. 8*

Fifteenth century French arm chair. *L'Art Pour Tous, Vol. 29*

Stuffed drawing room chair of black polished wood with gilt ornaments. *Workshop, Vol. 7*

Modern

The history of civilization is mirrored in the history of furniture. No other article of interior decoration is as sensitive to social change as the chair. Seating has undergone a metamorphosis—from rude bench, to throne, to easy chair. These changes resulted from a multitude of pressures extant at different periods of history.

The chairs of today reflect the technological advancements as well as the social tenor of the times. New materials and new techniques available to designers have allowed the form of the chair to vary. Chair design today runs the gamut from the economical lines of the molded plastic seat, to the luxurious comfort of the contour chair. Whatever its forms, simplicity of line marks the modern chair.

Advancements in communication and transportation have eliminated the insular development of parochial styles. In sharp contrast to their predecessors, furniture designers of the modern age work in an atmosphere of global influences unrestricted by national boundaries.

Hart □

Danish folding chair with oak legs
and rattan back and seat.
Catalog of the Unusual □

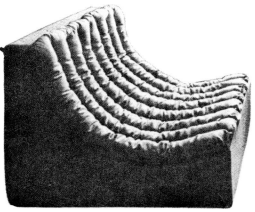

Scoop chair of solid foam fitted
with reversible cushion.
Catalog of the Unusual □

Danish arm chair of light oak with caned
seat. *Catalog of the Unusual* □

Danish teakwood chair with tilt back rest.
Catalog of the Unusual □

Danish swivel chair.
Catalog of the Unusual □

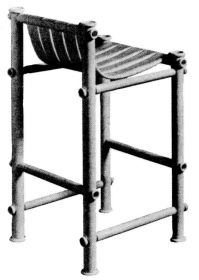

Bar stool of interlocking polyvinyl tubing with
acrilan sling seat. *Catalog of the Unusual* □

Lounge chair and ottoman of interlocking polyvinyl tubing with acrilan sling seat.
Catalog of the Unusual. □

Unusual Chairs

The chair, being the most common piece of furniture that exists, has inevitably produced many eccentric designs. A number of unusual forms have developed from the plain, garden variety of four-legged seats.

On the following pages, you will find a folding rocker, a bed chair which elongates into a sleeping apparatus, a swinging chair, and a chair which simulates a beer barrel, among other species. These are only a few of the manifold eccentric forms one meets with today.

Undoubtedly, the chair will continue to assume shapes and constructions not in our present imaginations—chairs which will delight and amaze future generations.

Hexagonal chair with petit point back and seat. *Hart* □

L'Art Pour Tous, Vol. 11

Black vinyl swivel rocker.
Catalog of the Unusual □

Silver chair, circa 1700.
Connoisseur, Vol. 14 □

Oriental monk's chair of rosewood.
Catalog of the Unusual □

Ashwood chair with untreated rope back of Danish design. *Catalog of the Unusual* □

Unusual Chairs continued

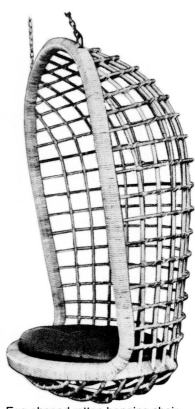

Egg-shaped rattan hanging chair.
Catalog of the Unusual □

Solid mahogany folding rocker. *Catalog of the Unusual.* □

Child's elephant chair of carved
rosewood has ivory toenails,
eyes and tusks. *Catalog of the
Unusual* □

Hand cast aluminum replica of a
seventeenth century chair. *Catalog of
the Unusual* □

Percival conversational ottoman. *Harper's*

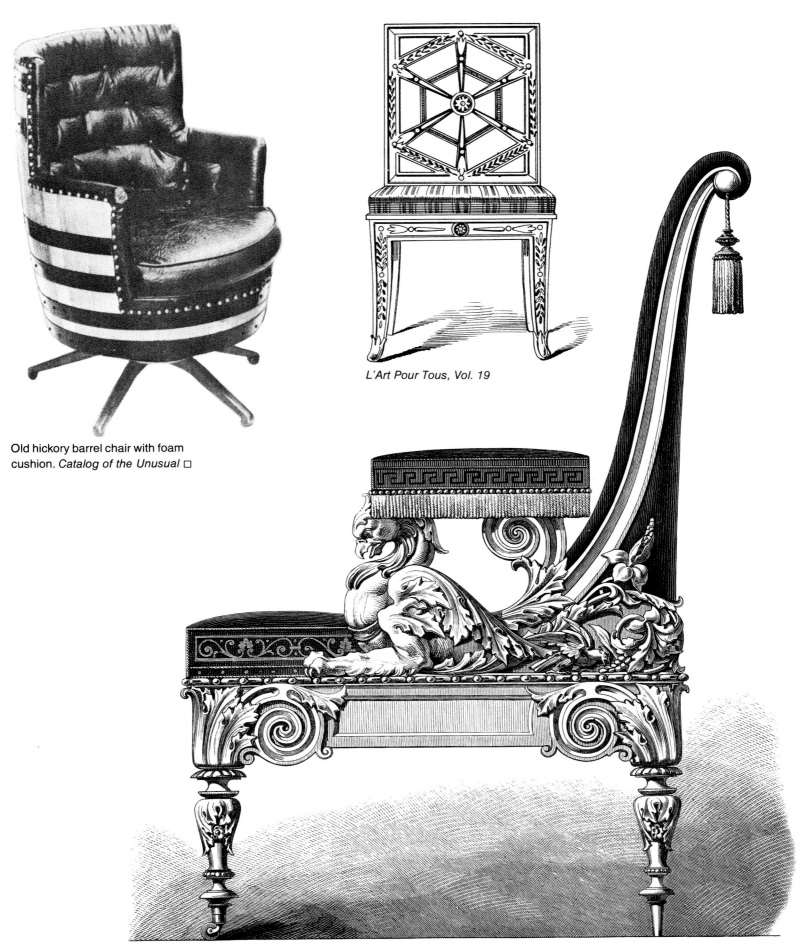

Old hickory barrel chair with foam
cushion. *Catalog of the Unusual* □

L'Art Pour Tous, Vol. 19

Nineteenth century chair of German design. *Workshop, 1870*

Unusual Chairs continued

Bed chair. *Old Furniture Book* □

Nelson's chair designed by Sheraton. *History of Furniture*

Seventeenth century Spanish chair of turned wood. *L'Art Pour Tous, Vol. 33*

Van Riebeck's chair made of African wood with caned seat. *Connoisseur, Vol. 25* □

Old oak trap chair. *Connoisseur, Vol. 8* ◻

Steel chair at Longford Castle, Wiltshire, England. *History of Furniture*

Steel rocker with vinyl back and seat cushions. *Catalog of the Unusual* ◻

Seats of Power

Furniture reflects the social, political, and cultural environment in which it is created. Perhaps no other piece of furniture has been as indicative of change as the chair. In many cases, the will of a mighty one has not only shaped the history of his nation, but also the chair upon which he sat.

Presented here are some interesting examples of chairs that were owned or used by some of the most famous and influential people in history: George Washington, Napoleon, Anne Boleyn, Robert Burns, Peter Paul Reubens, and Voltaire, among others.

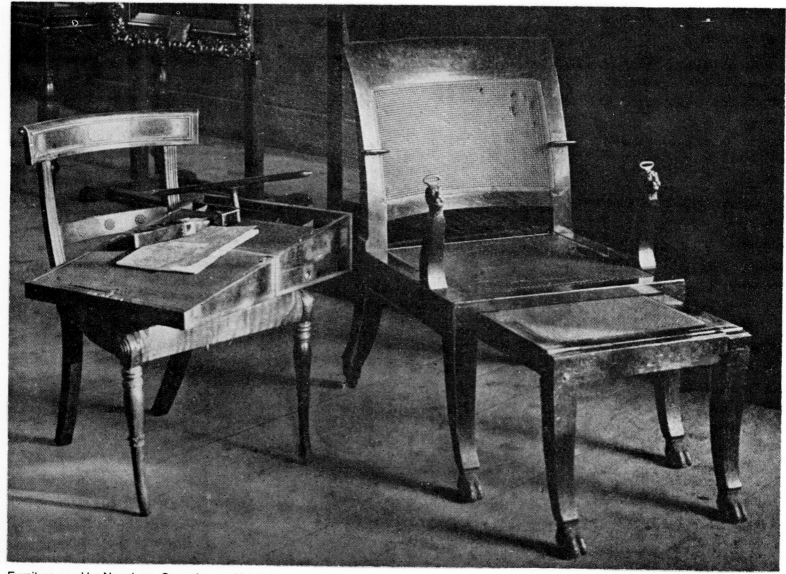

Furniture used by Napoleon. *Connoisseur, Vol. 8* □

Peter Paul Reubens' chair. *Harper's*

Chair used by Thomas Jefferson while writing the Declaration of Independence. *Furniture of Our Forefathers* □

Chair used by Nathaniel Hawthorne. *Furniture of Our Forefathers* □

Arm chair in which Voltaire died. *Harper's*

Seats of Power continued

Coronation chair of George IV. *Litchfield* □

Rush-bottom chair belonging to the Lincoln family. *Connoisseur,*

Chair occupied by the chairman of the Republican National Convention of 1860. *Harper's*

Four chairs from the River Room, Mount Vernon. The center left chair belonged to Benjamin Franklin. *Furniture of Our Forefathers*

Dagobert's chair. *Harper's*

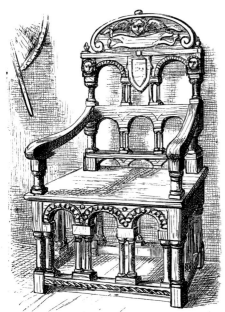

Chair made from the wood of a ship used by Sir Francis Drake. *Harper's*

Chair owned by Carver, the first governor of Plymouth Colony. *Century*

Chair in which Robert Burns was nursed. *Leslie's*

Chair used by William Shakespeare. *Leslie's*

Cromwell's arm chair. *Decorative Furniture*

William Penn's chair. *Furniture of Our Forefathers*

Walnut chair belonging to Sir William Gooch, Governor of Virginia 1727-1747. *Furniture of Our Forefathers*

Cardinal Wolsey's chair. *Connoisseur, Vol. 14* □

Seats of Power continued

Moliere's chair at Pezenzas.
Leslie's

Lord Nelson's chair, designed by Sheraton.
History of Furniture

Chair used by John Adams.
Furniture of Our Forefathers

Arm chair used by George Washington
in Virginia. *Century*

Chair owned by William Penn.
Furniture of Our Forefathers

Carved walnut chair belonging to
Michaelangelo. *Litchfield*

Chair belonging to Hogarth. *Connoisseur, Vol. 1*

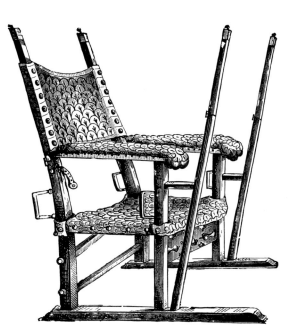

Sedan chair of Charles V. *Litchfield*

William Shakepeare's chair.
History of Furniture

De Witt Clinton's chair. *Harper's*

Benjamin Franklin's library chair (left), with the seat turned up to form a step ladder. *Furniture of Our Forefathers* ☐

GLOSSARY

ball foot (bun foot) flattened ball form used as a foot in England during the seventeenth century. This convention was replaced by the bracket foot.

ball and claw foot first used in Oriental furniture, the original claw was that of a dragon. This conventionalized form was redesigned to represent either a lion's or eagle's claw when employed by English furniture designers. This foot style was popular throughout the Chippendale era.

baluster (banister) small, slender turned column, usually widened in the middle and used for the uprights in chair backs.

banister (baluster) small, slender turned column, usually widened in the middle and used for the uprights of chair backs.

bead molding (cockle bead molding) small, semi-circular molding adorned with round or oval elements

boulle work tortoise-shell and metal inlay popular in eighteenth century France. This decorative device takes its name from its inventor, Andre Charles Boulle.

bun foot (ball foot) flattened ball form used as a foot in England during the seventeenth century. This convention was replaced by the bracket foot.

cabochon convex or concave, round or oval surface enclosed within an ornamental border. Chippendale's decorative motifs often took this form.

cabriole leg design of a chair leg with protruding rounded knee and concaved ankle. This leg style is characteristic of chairs designed during the William and Mary and Queen Anne periods.

cartouche ornamental device of irregular form enclosing a plain, central surface.

caryatid conventionalized human form used as a supporting member in architecture of furniture design.

certosina (intarsia, tarsia) inlaying technique where the background wood is cut away and the space filled with a contrasting material. This favored ornament of Renaissance Italy usually employed ivory or fine bone as the contrasting material and was used to depict still lifes or scenes from nature.

chamfer beveled cut of a corner.

chased work a process of ornamenting metal by indenting with a blunt instrument such as a hammer.

club foot (duck-bill foot, pad foot) plain, flat foot introduced into English furniture design during the early eighteenth century and used until the beginning of the nineteenth century.

cockle bead molding (bead molding) small, semi-circular molding adorned with round or oval elements.

cresting carving on the top rail of a chair. This feature is characteristic of English chairs designed during the Restoration.

curule square seated chair with "X" shaped legs derived from early Roman forms. This design was especially popular in Italy and Spain during the Renaissance.

cyma curve a double or compound "S" curve. It is the characteristic line of the cabriole leg and the carved splat connecting the top and seat rails during the Queen Anne period.

dovetail a method of joining wood pieces by interlocking wedge-shaped tenons and spaces.

duck-bill foot (club foot, pad foot) plain, flat foot introduced into English furniture design during the early eighteenth century and used until the beginning of the nineteenth century.

fasces a bundle of rods from which an axe or blade projects. They were carried in processions before Roman magistrates as symbols of authority.

festoon decorative device consisting of a series of scallops, forming a rope, chain, or drapery effect.

Flemish scroll baroque form of the sixteenth century and seventeenth century in which the characteristic curve is broken by an interposed angle.

fluting channeling or grooving cut into a flat surface.

fretwork (lattice work) interlace, ornamental work, either perforated or applied to a solid background. These designs are typical of Chinese Chippendale chair backs.

gilding ornamentation of raised decoration by the use of gold coloring preparations.

hoof foot foot style resembling the hoof of an animal. Often used with the cabriole leg, it was introduced into England at the end of the seventeenth century.

inlay decorative method using contrasting woods and metals set into a solid base.

intarsia (certosina, tarsia) inlaying technique where the background wood is cut away and the space filled with contrasting material. This favored ornament of Renaissance Italy usually employed ivory or fine bone as the contrasting material and was used to depict still lifes or scenes from nature.

japanning imitation lacquer work developed in Europe. This type of high luster finish was popular during the Georgian period.

join the fixing together of two structural elements of furniture. Many methods have been used in chair construction including mortise and tenon, and tongue and groove joins.

lacquer varnish-like finish for woodwork particularly suited to decorative overpainting. Of Oriental origin, the lac is obtained from the resin of trees indigenous to the East. The high gloss surface is produced through the application of many thin coats of lacquer to wooden surfaces.

lattice work (fretwork) interlaced, ornamental work, either perforated or applied to a solid background. These designs are typical of Chinese Chippendale chair backs.

marquetry inlay of wood veneer in designs representing flowers, garlands, landscapes, etc. This later form of inlay is a development of Italian intarsia revived during the Renaissance.

mortise and tenon method of joining structural elements in which a protruding piece (tenon) is fitted into a space (mortise) cut to receive that piece. This joining technique was in general use during colonial times in America.

mount ornamental metal work.

ormolu decorative mounts of gilded brass or copper popular in France during the eighteenth century.

pad foot (club foot, duck-bill foot) plain, flat foot introduced into English furniture design during the early eighteenth century and used until the beginning of the nineteenth century.

reeding parallel lines of convex relief wood carving. This type of ornamental wood carving is the opposite of fluting, which is concave.

settle an article of furniture for seating developed from the chest. The settle usually has a locker underneath the seat portion for storage.

spade foot four-sided, tapering block foot. This foot style was used extensively by Hepplewhite and Sheraton.

splat central portion of a chair back which connects the top rail and the seat rail.

spoon back chair back that is shaped to fit human contours. This back style was developed during the Queen Anne period.

strap-work a narrow, ornamental band consisting of a repeated pattern of crossed or interlaced elements.

stretcher underbraces which connect the legs of a chair. They disappeared from chair design about 1730 and were reintroduced during Hepplewhite's career.

tarsia (intarsia, certosina) inlaying technique where the background wood is cut away and the space filled with contrasting material. This favored ornament of Renaissance Italy usually employed ivory or fine bone as the contrasting material and was used to depict still lifes or scenes from nature.

top rail topmost crosspiece of a chair back.

tracery ornamental work of interlaced lines typical of Gothic cathedral windows.

veneer thin layer of richly grained wood applied to a plain, solid wood surface.

wainscot chair characteristic Tudor or Jacobean chair. Usually constructed of oak, it had a box bottom and the back carved to match the chests and cupboards of the period.

SOURCES

CATALOG OF THE UNUSUAL. Hart, Harold H. New York: Hart Publishing Co., Inc., 1973.

CENTURY DICTIONARY; full title, *The Century Dictionary and Cyclopedia* (twelve vol.). New York: The Century Company, 1889-1913.

CENTURY MAGAZINE; full title, *The Century Illustrated Monthly Magazine.* New York: The Century Company, vol. 1, 2, 3, 6, 7, 8, 9, 11, 13; individual issues 1883, 1884, 1885, 1888, 1889, 1890, 1891, 1892, 1894, 1895, 1896, 1901.

CONNOISSEUR, THE; full title, *The Connoisseur, An Illustrated Magazine for Collectors.* London: Otto Ltd., vol. 1, 2, 3, 4, 5, 6, 7, 8, 9, 10, 11, 12, 13, 14, 15, 16, 21, 25, 36, 45.

DECORATIVE FURNITURE; full title, *Decorative Furniture of the Seventeeth, Eighteenth, and Nineteenth Centuries.* Hackell, W.H. London: 1902.

DRAWING & DESIGN; full title, *Drawing & Design, The Magazine of Taste.* New series 1, 2, 3, 4, 5, 6, 7, 8, 9, 10, 11, 12.

FURNITURE OF OUR FOREFATHERS, THE. Singleton, Esther. New York: Doubleday, Page, & Co., 1901.

HARPER'S; full title, *Harper's New Monthly Magazine.* New York: Harper & Brothers, vol. 2, 3, 5, 8, 10, 16, 17, 18, 19, 20, 21, 22, 27, 30, 31, 32, 36, 37, 38, 40, 41, 42, 43, 44, 45, 46, 47, 48, 49, 50, 51, 53, 54, 56, 57, 58, 61, 64, 65, 66, 67, 68, 69, 70, 71, 74, 75, 77, 88, 89, 103.

HART. Private collection of Harold H. Hart.

HISTORY OF FURNITURE, A. Jacquemart, Albert. London: Reeves and Turner, no date.

INDUSTRY OF NATIONS; full title, *Chefs-D'Oeuvre of the Industrial Arts.* Burty, Phillipe. New York: D. Appleton and Co., 1869.

L'ART POUR TOUS; full title, *L'Art Pour Tous, Encyclopedie de l'Art Industriel et Decoratif.* Reiber, Emile, ed. Paris: A. Morel et

LESLIE'S; full title, *Frank Leslie's Popular Monthly Magazine.* New York: Frank Leslie Publishing House, vol. 10, 12, 13, 14, 15, 16, 17, 21, 23, 24, 25, 26, 29, 31, 32, 34, 35, 36, 38.

LITCHFIELD; full title, *An Illustrated History of Furniture from the Earliest to the Present Time.* Litchfield, Frederick. London: Truslove & Shirley, 1892.

MONTGOMERY WARD CATALOG; full title, *Montgomery Ward & Company Catalog No. 57, Catalog and Buyers' Guide, Spring and Summer.* Chicago: Montgomery Ward & Co., 1895.

OLD FURNITURE BOOK, THE. Moore, N. Hudson. New York: Frederick A. Stokes & Co., 1903.

PERIOD STYLES; full title, *An Introduction to the Period Styles of England and France.* Cole, Herbert. Manchester: The Sutherland Publishing Company, Ltd., no date.

SEARS CATALOG; full title, *The Sears, Roebuck Catalog.* Chicago: The Sears, Roebuck Company, 1902.

SPIERS & POND'S CATALOG. London: Spiers & Pond's Stores, Ltd., Nov. 1903-Oct. 1904.

SUNDAY BOOK; full title, *The Pictorial Sunday Book.* Kitto, Dr. John, ed. London: The London Printing & Publishing Company, Ltd., no date.

WORKSHOP; full title, *The Workshop, A Monthly Journal Devoted to Progress of the Useful Arts.* Baumer, W., I. Schnorr, eds. New York: E. Steiger, etc., 1868-1883.

ZELL'S; full title, *Zell's Encyclopedia and Atlas* (four vol.). Colange, Leo, ed. Philadelphia: T. Ellwood Zell, Davis & Co., 1880.

INDEX

INDEX continued